Study Guide

for Reed's

Cognition

Theory and Applications

Sixth Edition

Linda S. Buyer
Governors State University

THOMSON

WADSWORTH

Australia • Canada • Mexico • Singapore • Spain • United Kingdom • United States

For more information about our products, contact us at:
Thomson Learning Academic Resource Center
1-800-423-0563

For permission to use material from this text, contact us by:
Phone: 1-800-730-2214
Fax: 1-800-731-2215
Web: http://www.thomsonrights.com

Wadsworth/Thomson Learning
10 Davis Drive
Belmont, CA 94002-3098
USA

Asia
Thomson Learning
5 Shenton Way #01-01
UIC Building
Singapore 068808

Australia/New Zealand
Thomson Learning
102 Dodds Street
Southbank, Victoria 3006
Australia

Canada
Nelson
1120 Birchmount Road
Toronto, Ontario M1K 5G4
Canada

Europe/Middle East/South Africa
Thomson Learning
High Holborn House
50/51 Bedford Row
London WC1R 4LR
United Kingdom

Latin America
Thomson Learning
Seneca, 53
Colonia Polanco
11560 Mexico D.F.
Mexico

Spain/Portugal
Paraninfo
Calle/Magallanes, 25
28015 Madrid, Spain

STUDY GUIDE FOR REED'S COGNITION
TABLE OF CONTENTS

SHORT CONTENTS

STUDY GUIDE FOR REED'S COGNITION
TABLE OF CONTENTS

CONTENTS

STUDY GUIDE FOR REED'S COGNITION
TABLE OF CONTENTS

STUDY GUIDE FOR REED'S COGNITION
TABLE OF CONTENTS

PREFACE

This study guide is intended to ease the task of mastering cognitive psychology as set out in Stephen K. Reed's *Cognition: Theory and Applications (6th Edition)*. The earliest version of this study guide was written for my students at Governors State University in response to complaints from my students that Reed's textbook was "too hard." As I saw it, I had two choices. I could stop using a textbook that I think contains the best summary of cognitive psychology for undergraduate students and choose a book that I liked less and my students liked more or I could find a way to make the book that I liked so much easier for my students. I chose the latter course of action. Since I wrote the first version of the study guide, my students no longer complain that Reed's text is too difficult.

The first section of the study guide contains "Do-it-Your Experiments" that all have applications to increasing studying efficiency. Each of the experiments demonstrates one strategy that can be used to increase your comprehension and/or memory of to-be-learned materials without increasing the amount of time you spend trying to learn the material. I hope that these self-demonstrations convince you to apply these strategies while you study Reed's *Cognition: Theory and Application (6th Edition)*. For additional experimental results that have direct applications to more efficient study, see Nelson and Dunlosky's (1994) Judgments-of-Learning (J-O-L) experiment on pages 105-106 in *Chapter 5: Long-term Memory* or the section on Transfer Appropriate Processing on pages 145-148 in *Chapter 6: Memory Codes*. The self-demonstrations begin on the following page.

The second section of the study guide contains outlines of each chapter of the textbook and self-test study questions for you to use to evaluate your understanding of the chapter material. If you bring the outlines to class with you, this will reduce the need to take notes and listen to your instructor simultaneously. You will be able to focus your attention on listening to the instructor and understanding what he or has to say about cognitive psychology and only have to make marginal notes relating to the instructor's examples or additions to the text content. For more information about overload and the attention process, see the section covering Kahneman's Capacity Theory on pages 53-55 in *Chapter 3: Attention*. Italicized words in the chapter outlines are from the "Key Terms" lists in the related chapters. The "Key Terms" lists give the page reference for each of the italicized words.

Following each chapter's outline is a "Practice Questions" section. Each "Practice Questions" section contains multiple-choice, true/false, and essay questions that will help you to evaluate your understanding of the chapter's content. The "Outlines and Practice Questions" section begins on page 1.

The last section of the study guide identifies the correct answers to the multiple-choice and true/false practice questions. It also gives page references to the location of the correct answers in the textbook. The "Answers to Practice Questions" section begins on page 159.

I hope that you will find this study guide as useful as my students do.

Linda S. Buyer

EXPERIMENT 1: GETTING MORE BANG FROM YOUR "STUDY BUCK"

Study efficiently rather than longer by taking advantage of the "Release from Proactive Interference" phenomenon. The "release from proactive interference" phenomenon (Wickens, 1963) is described fully on pages 74-76 in *Chapter Four: Short-term and Working Memory*.

For this Demonstration you will Need the Following:

- 1 sheet of paper, torn into 9 equal parts (each of which needs to be large enough on which to write 3 words). Number the pieces of paper from 1 to 9.
- A pen or pencil
- A stop watch or any timing device that will count seconds
- A participant who is willing to take a series of memory tests
- The table shown below. (The table contains the nine lists that will be used during the experiment.)

LIST	TO-BE-RECALLED WORDS	3-DIGIT NUMBER
1	MAGNOLIA, GLADIOLA, LAVENDER	516
2	LILY, BLUE BELLS, LILAC	405
3	PANSY, DAFFODIL, DAISY	745
4	ROSE, JASMINE, VIOLET	954
5	HISTORY, PSYCHOLOGY, DRAMA	820
6	ENGLISH, MUSIC, ALGEBRA	631
7	PHYSICS, BIOLOGY, ART	267
8	CHEMISTRY, CALCULUS, SOCIOLOGY	564
9	WASHINGTON, LINCOLN, ROOSEVELT	243

To Conduct the Experiment:

(Read the instructions from beginning to end <u>before</u> beginning the demonstration.)

1. Tell your participant that you are going to read him or her several lists each of which have three words. At the end of each list, you will read a 3-digit number. When your participant hears the number, he or she should begin to count backwards by 3's. (For example, 99, 96, 93, 90, 87, 84, 81, 78, 75, 72, 69, etc.). Also tell the participant that you want him or her to continue to

count backwards until you clap your hands. Tell the participant that he or she should write down the three words on the list when you clap your hands. The words from List 1 should be written on the slip of paper that is labeled "1," etc.
2. Give your friend an opportunity to practice counting backward by 3's now, before you begin the experiment. Have your participant start counting backward from 99.
3. Use the stopwatch to make sure that the participant counts backwards for 20 seconds.
4. When 20 seconds has elapsed, clap your hands.
5. Give the participant the nine numbered pieces of paper and the pen or pencil. Read the lists to the participant one at a time. For each list, read the to-be-recalled words in a monotone at the pace of one word per second. Immediately following your reading of the list, read the 3-digit number printed to the right of the list. Have the participant count backward by 3's from that number until 20 seconds have passed. When 20 seconds have elapsed, clap your hands and have the participant write down the to-be-recalled words on the piece of paper that has the same number as the list.
6. After presenting all nine lists, score your participant's recall. You can use the graph shown below to see your results. Place an "X" at the intersection of each list's number and the number of words the participant correctly recalled from that list. You can use Figure 4.4 on page 75 as a model of how to translate your data into the graph.

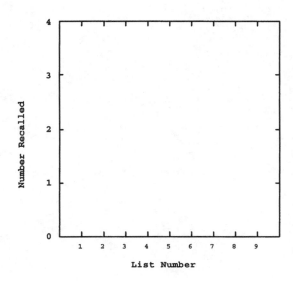

Application of the Demonstration to Studying:

The "take home" message from this demonstration is that memory improves when one switches from items that all share one semantic content to items that share a different semantic content. You can use this knowledge to study more efficiently (remember more from the same amount of study time). Instead of studying for a single class for long periods of time, study for each class for a short time and then, to take advantage of "release from proactive inhibition," switch and study for another class. With the exact same amount of time spent studying each week, you should be able to remember more of the material if you study every class each day that you study, than if you study each class all in one day.

EXPERIMENT 2: MEMORY TRICKS

Here's another demonstration that you can study more efficiently rather than longer. Mnemonics (memory "tricks") are described more fully on pages 161-163 in *Chapter Seven: Imagery*.

For this Demonstration you will Need the Following:

- Someone who is willing to spend approximately 20 minutes learning a "trick" to improve his/her memory
- A pen or pencil
- A stop watch or any timing device that will count seconds
- Three lists shown below and on the next page:

The practice list:

ITEM NUMBER	PROFESSIONS
1	Accountant
2	Psychologist
3	Teacher
4	Sculptor
5	Lawyer
6	Judge
7	Carpenter
8	Painter
9	Doctor
10	Singer

The Peg Word list: **The grocery list:**

NUMBER	PEG WORDS	ITEM NUMBER	GROCERIES
1	is a bun	1	Coffee
2	is a shoe	2	Apples
3	is a tree	3	Chicken
4	is a door	4	Cookies
5	is a hive	5	Zucchini
6	is sticks	6	Pie
7	is heaven	7	Corn
8	is a gate	8	Bread
9	is a vine	9	Popcorn
10	is a hen	10	Lemons

To Conduct the Experiment:

(Read the instructions from beginning to end <u>before</u> beginning the demonstration.)

1. Allow the participant 5 minutes to try to memorize the practice list. Tell the participant that it is important to remember both the professions and the number assigned to each one. Read the list aloud, one profession/number pair at a time. Allow 30 seconds for each pair.
2. Now, get a baseline measure of your participant's ability to remember items in order. For each of the following memory tests, write down the number of items the person gets correct. Ask the participant (a) to recall the list in forward order -- without saying the numbers, (b) to recall the list in backward order -- again without saying the numbers, (c) to identify the 5th, 3rd, and 9th words on the list, and (d) to give the correct numbers for 'Judge,' 'Painter,' and 'Sculptor.'
3. Now, have the participant memorize the "Peg Word" list. Allow the participant to take as long as he or she wants to do so. Before continuing, test the participant to make sure he or she has memorized the peg words, e.g., "What's the peg word for 7?" and "What number goes with door?"
4. Tell the participant that you are going to present another ten-item list. Tell the participant to create a vivid mental image of the list item interacting with the appropriate word. Say the following, "For example, if the first word on the list is 'gorilla,' you might imagine either a gorilla holding a hamburger on a bun or a 'gorilla sandwich' on a huge bun. It very important the list word and peg

interact in the image (they shouldn't just be side-by-side). It is also important the images be distinct (not similar to one another)."

5. Allow the participant 5 minutes to try to memorize the grocery list by associating it with the peg word list. Tell the participant that it is important to remember both the grocery items and the number assigned to each one. Read the list aloud, one grocery item/number pair at a time. Allow 30 seconds for each pair.

6. Now, measure the effect of using the peg words on your participant's ability to remember items in order. Again, for each of the memory tests, write down the number of items the person gets correct. Ask the participant (a) to recall the list in forward order -- without saying the numbers, (b) to recall the list in backward order -- again without saying the numbers, (c) to identify the 5th, 3rd, and 9th words on the list, and (d) to give the correct numbers for 'Pie,' 'Bread,' and 'Cookies.'

7. Fill in the table below using the data you collected.

ITEMS CORRECTLY RECALLED

RECALL TASK	NUMBER ITEMS CORRECTLY RECALLED	
	Professions	Groceries
Forward		
Backward		
5th, 3rd, and 9th		
Gave correct #s		

Application of the Demonstration to Studying:

The "take home" message from this demonstration is that mnemonics, although they require some amount of extra effort initially, greatly improve your ability to recall the to-be-learned information. Certain topics in college courses require the memorization of lists of one kind or another. The same amount of time spent studying can be put to more effective use if you use mnemonics than if you simply use rote rehearsal to memorize the list. Suggestions for the use of the pegwords: memorizing the "Table of Elements" for a chemistry class (you can create more than one image per peg word); learning, in order, the names of the U. S. Presidents; or memorizing the parts of a speech you have to give. Like the Peg Word technique, the Method of Loci (using a sequence of familiar location, e.g., buildings you pass on your way to work) is most useful if information needs to be memorized in order, for example the historical events leading up to World War II. The "Key Word" mnemonic (described on pages 161-163 of the text) can be used when one needs to learn the association between two items. For example, the Key Word mnemonic can be used for learning translations of foreign words, for associating theories with those who proposed them, or connecting the names and faces of new acquaintances.

EXPERIMENT 3: IMPROVING READING COMPREHENSION

The effects of prior context on comprehension are fully described in pages 274-277 of *Chapter Eleven: Comprehension and Memory for Text.*

For this Demonstration you will Need the Following:
- 1 person who is willing to listen to same paragraph twice and to try three times to recall the paragraph
- 3 sheets of notebook paper
- A pen or pencil
- A stop watch or any timing device that will count seconds
- The following paragraph: (Don't worry if it doesn't make sense until after you read the directions.)

> (1) Before you start, it's a good idea to assemble all of the (2) components and (3) measuring devices that you will need. (4) After everything is assembled, read all of the instructions, otherwise the effort might be in vain. (5) Make sure you do not deviate from the instructions, doing may so cause a failure to make the appropriate ascent. (6) Turn on the energy-producing device. (7) Put the dry components in a (8) large container. (9) Add in the remaining components. (10) Stir until the texture is that of library paste. (11) Lubricate the container you intend to use when you attempt ascent. (12) The container you use to heat the mixture should hold approximately three times the volume of the mixture, otherwise an appropriate ascent cannot occur. (13) Put the mixture into the container and (14) apply energy for the time specified in the directions included with the product.

To Conduct the Experiment:

(Read the instructions from beginning to end <u>before</u> beginning the demonstration.)

1. Tell the participant that you are going to read him or her a short paragraph and that you will test the participant's memory for the passage shortly after the passage is presented. Add that at the end of the paragraph, you will read a number and that you want the participant to count backward by 3's from the number until you clap your hands.

2. Give your friend an opportunity to practice counting backward by 3's now, before you begin the experiment. Have your participant start counting backward from 99.

3. When 20 seconds has elapsed, clap your hands. Tell the participant that "this will be your cue to write down everything you remember from the paragraph."

4. <u>No Context Condition</u>: Read the paragraph above in a monotone at a steady pace. Do NOT read the imbedded numbers. Those are included for you to score the participant's memory performance.

5. Have the participant count backward from 498 by 3's until 20 seconds has elapsed. Clap your hands.

6. Have the participant write down every thing that he or she can remember from the passage. Count how many of the 23 numbered concepts mentioned in the paragraph are mentioned in the recall report.

7. <u>Context After Condition</u>: Now, tell the participant that the title of the paragraph is "Using a Mix to Bake a Cake" and ask the participant to once again write down everything that he or she can remember from the paragraph. Again count how many of the numbered concepts are included in the report.

8. <u>Context Before Condition</u>: Read the paragraph the same way you did the first time.

9. Have the participant count backward from 797 by 3's until 20 seconds have elapsed. Clap your hands.

10. Ask the participant to write down everything that he or she can remember from the paragraph. Again count how many of the numbered concepts are included in the report. You can use the table below to organize your results.

NUMBER OF CONCEPTS CORRECTLY RECALLED

	CONDITION		
	No Context	Context After	Context Before
Correct Recall			

Application of the Demonstration to Studying:

The "take home" message from this demonstration is that establishing a meaningful context for abstract material makes the material easier to understand and remember. You can apply this knowledge to reading your text more efficiently. Start by reading the Preface and the Table(s) of Contents. What topics will be covered? What level of student was the text written for? Is there a Glossary? In order to construct a context for each chapter's material, begin by reading the chapter outline, if there is one. Then read the chapter summary. Then, if there are any, read the 'End-of-the-Chapter' questions. If you approach each chapter in this way, by the time you begin reading the chapter, you will already have a good idea of what the chapter's about and what its author thinks are the important points. Having this knowledge should make it easier for you to comprehend the to-be-learned chapter contents.

CHAPTER 1: INTRODUCTION

I. Information Processing Approach

Input   Response
↓↓↓↓   ↑↑↑↑

| Sensory Stores | ┈► | Filter | ↔ | Pattern Recognition | ↔ | Selection | ↔ | Short-Term Memory | ↔ | Long-Term Memory |

A. One sensory store for each sense (i.e., sight, hearing, smell, taste and touch)

B. Attention is a function of both *filter* and *selection* processes.

C. Short-term Memory has <u>both</u> limited duration and limited capacity.

D. Long-term Memory has <u>neither</u> limited duration nor limited capacity.

   1. Top-down processing (information flows from LTM to Sensory Store)

   2. Bottom-up processing (information flows from Sensory Store to LTM)

E. "Higher" cognitive skills (e.g., decision making and problem solving)

   1. are <u>not included</u> in the model of human information processing shown above

   2. <u>depend on</u> the processes shown in the model above (e.g., playing chess requires pattern recognition)

II. The Growth of Cognitive Psychology

A. Early Positive Influences
1. William James's (1890) *Principles of Psychology*
2. Wolfgang Kohler's (1925) *The Mentality of Apes*
3. F. Bartlett's (1932) *Remembering: A Study in Experimental and Social Psychology*

B. Early Negative Influences: John Watson's (1924) *Behaviorism* (S-R approach)

C. In the **Mid- to late-1950's** computers were viewed as a model of information processing

D. George Miller's (1956) *Psychological Review* article, "The magical number seven, plus or minus two: some limits on our capacity for processing information"

E. Donald Broadbent's (1958) proposal of the "Filter Model" to explain attention

F. George Sperling's (1960) discovery of iconic memory store

G. Higher Cognitive Processes
1. Artificial Intelligence (programming computers to perform tasks requiring "intelligence") led to ideas about how computer simulation techniques could be used to create and test models of human behavior.
2. Newell and Simon (1956; 1972) proposed the Information Processing Model (see Section I above).
3. Noam Chomsky (1957) proposed Transformational Grammar.
4. Miller, Galanter, & Pribram's (1960) *Plans and the Structure of Behavior* (in which they proposed TOTE units) was affected by both Newell & Simon's work and that of Chomsky.

III. Cognition's Relation to Other Fields

A. Cognitive Psychology

1. includes perception, attention, learning, memory, language, reasoning, problem solving, and decision making
2. has influenced both educational psychology and social psychology
3. is used to solve applied problems (e.g., to design better problem solving and memory strategies or to increase the accuracy of eyewitness testimony)

B. Cognitive Science is the study of intelligence wherever it may be found (emphasis is on intelligent behavior as computation)

C. Cognitive Neuroscience provides data that can be used to evaluate cognitive theories

1. Magnetic Resonance Imaging (MRI) and functional Magnetic Resonance Imaging (fMRI)
2. Positron Emission Tomography (PET)
3. Event-related Potentials (ERP)

IV. Organization of this Book

PART 1	PART 2	PART 3
Information Processing Stages	Representation and Organization of Knowledge	Complex ("Higher") Cognitive Skills
• Pattern Recognition • Attention • Short-term Memory • Long-term Memory	• Memory Codes (visual and verbal) • Organization of Long-term Memory	• Language • Text Comprehension • Problem Solving • Expertise and Creativity • Decision making

CHAPTER 1: PRACTICE QUESTIONS (Answers and page references are on p. 165.)

Multiple Choice Questions: For each question, circle the single, best alternative.

1. Which term was included in Neisser's definition of cognitive psychology?

   a. reduced
   b. recovered
   c. used
   d. all of the above

2. What is the correct order of stages in an information processing model?

   a. selection - LTM - STM
   b. LTM - STM - selection
   c. selection - STM - LTM
   d. STM - selection - LTM

3. Which stage in the information processing model is most affected by the attentional filter?

   a. sensory store
   b. pattern recognition
   c. STM
   d. LTM

4. Short-term memory has

   a. limited capacity.
   b. limited duration.
   c. both *a* and *b*
   d. neither *a* nor *b*

5. Miller, Galanter, and Pribram contributed the idea of the _____ to cognitive psychology.

   a. TOTE (Test-Operate-Test-Exit) unit
   b. JND (just noticeable difference)
   c. sensory stores
   d. attentional filter

6. The field of study called artificial intelligence focuses on

   a. programming computers to perform intellectually demanding tasks.
   b. programming computers to solve problems exactly like human beings.
   c. programming computers to have emotions.
   d. all of the above

7. Cognitive neuroscience is the

   a. interdisciplinary study of cognition through psychology, philosophy, linguistics, etc.
   b. study of perception, attention, language, reasoning, problem solving, decision making, etc.
   c. study of the relation between cognitive processes and brain activities.
   d. none of the above

8. Event-related potentials are used to

   a. obtain precise temporal information about the time course of mental operations.
   b. measure blood flow in the brain.
   c. measure which parts of the brain are used to perform various cognitive tasks.
   d. conduct PET and MRI research.

9. "Attention" is synonymous with which components of the Information- Processing model?

    a. sensory store and filter
    b. filter and selection
    c. pattern recognition and STM
    d. selection and STM

10. Positron emission tomography uses

    a. electrical activity from the scalp to provide temporal information about mental operations.
    b. magnetic fields to obtain pictures of brain structure.
    c. radioactive tracers to measure blood flow in the brain.
    d. CAT scans to obtain information about brain activity.

11. Bartlett (1932) contributed an early theory of _____ that is consistent with current views of cognitive psychology.

    a. problem solving
    b. attention
    c. memory
    d. decision making

12. Top-down processing is a description of which of the following?

    a. seeing a cat because that's the animal you expected to see
    b. seeing a cat because you're exposed to something that meows and has fur
    c. recognizing that a sound pattern is an unfamiliar word
    d. recognizing that the television is turned off

True-False Questions:

(T) F   1.   There is one sensory store for each of the five senses.

T (F)   2.   Reasoning is one of the "lower" cognitive skills.

T F   3.   The information processing model was proposed by Ulrich Neisser.

(T) F   4.   Selection is the process that determines whether an item from a sensory store will be recognized.

T F   5.   The "higher" cognitive processes are identified in the information processing model.

T F   6.   Psychologists are most interested in cognitive neuroscience when it can be used to test cognitive theories.

T F   7.   Evidence for the use of visual imagery comes from the observation that the same part of the brain is active when one is "looking" at a mental image and when one is looking at an external stimulus.

T F   8.   The "higher" cognitive processes that are covered in Part 3 of the textbook depend on the processes that make up the information processing model.

(T) F   9.   Cognitive science represents the attempt to create a unified theory of thought by bringing together many disciplines (e.g., linguistics, anthropology, psychology, philosophy).

T (F)   10.   A plan consists of an unordered string of TOTE units.

T (F)   11.   Bottom-up processing is superior to (better than) top-down processing.

Essay Questions:

1. Why do psychologists make a distinction between the "higher" and "lower" cognitive processes? Give two examples of each kind of process.

2. What are the stages in the Information Processing model? Describe each stage and its function(s).

CHAPTER 2: PATTERN RECOGNITION

I. **Describing Patterns:**
    A. Template Theories
    1. A template is a stored representation of a holistic, unanalyzed object.
    2. Input is compared to template by measuring overlap.
    3. Problems:
        a. Comparison requires two patterns to be in same orientation and position as well as same size
        b. Variability of input patterns
        c. Can't explain <u>how</u> patterns differ
    4. Evidence for the model comes from Phillip's (1974) experiment showing that the sensory store can be used for template matching <u>if</u> the interstimulus interval (ISI) is less than or equal to 300 msec.
    B. Feature Theories
    1. A feature is a very simple pattern, a fragment or component that can appear in combination with other features across a wide variety of stimulus patterns (e.g., many letters of the alphabet have a vertical feature).
    2. Whole patterns are recognized by breaking them into the features of which they are comprised.
    3. Evidence for:
        a. *Perceptual confusions* (matching errors, errors in same vs. different decisions, incorrect identification of tachistoscopically presented letters)
        b. Hubel and Weisel's (1962, 1963) Nobel Prize winning work on the visual system (certain cells only respond to certain kinds of stimuli)
        c. Learning/recognition can be facilitated by highlighting *distinctive features* (Egeland, 1975).

        d. Learning distinctive features can be difficult even for adults when the objects come from the same category.

    4. A problem with feature theory is that Townsend's (1971) data are better predicted by the template model than by a feature model.

C. Structural Theories

1. Extension of feature theories
2. Specify *relations* among features
3. Evidence for:
   a. Objects with identical features can produce different descriptions (Shepard, 1990).
   b. Biederman (1985) has shown that deleting information about the relations among features decreases recognition.
      i. Only 35 *geons* needed to describe objects in world (Biederman's Component model)
      ii. Faster and more accurate identifications when complementary images shared geons

II. Information Processing Stages
A. Partial-report technique

1. *Whole-report* procedure (report everything you see)
   a. In general, if there were fewer than 5 letters in the display, subjects could recall all of them.
   b. However, if the number of letters was increased, subjects still only reported an average of 4.5 letters correctly.
2. Somewhere in one (or more) of the stages involved in the processing of information, there was a *bottleneck*.
   a. Are we limited by our ability to <u>perceive</u> all of the available stimulation?
   b. Are we limited in our ability to <u>remember</u> all of the available stimulation?
3. Sperling designed the *partial-report* paradigm.
   a. Instead of reporting everything you saw in the display (as in the whole-report paradigm), a tone

       signaled which row of the display to report (3 rows, 4 letters each).

b. A high-pitched tone signaled that subjects were to report the top row, a medium tone indicated the middle row, and a low tone the bottom row.

c. The tone was sounded after the display when the letters were no longer visible.

d. However many letters were reported from the *cued* row should represent the number that could be reported from any one of the rows.

e. Separates the quantity of material <u>perceived</u> from the amount that one can <u>remember.</u>

4. Results:

    a. With no delay of tone, average subject could report 3 of the 4 letters in a row, thus implying that they had recognized 9 of the letters in the 12 item display.

    b. When tone was delayed by 150 msec, average subject correctly reported only 2.5 letters from row ($2.5 \times 3 = 7.5$).

    c. At 300 msec delay, subjects could only report 2 letters from the cued row ($2 \times 3 = 6$).

    d. At a 1 sec delay, subjects were reporting an average of 1.5 letters per row ($1.5 \times 3 = 4.5$). Note: This is exactly comparable to performance in the whole-report condition.

B. Sperling's Model

1. The components are: a *visual information store* (VIS), *scanning, rehearsal,* and an *auditory information store*.

2. Subjects use VIS to recognize the information in the cued row.

    a. When they heard the tone they selectively attended to the information in the cued row and tried to identify the letters in that row.

    b. VIS retains a *veridical* representation of the incoming stimulus for up to 1 second.

        c. Decay rate depends on factors such as intensity, contrast, duration, and on whether stimulus is followed by a second exposure (*visual masking*).

        d. Information in the VIS must be *scanned* in order for it to be recognized.

    3. *Rehearsal* and the *auditory information store (AIS)* are used to retain the items until recall is required.

C. Rumelhart's Model

    1. Rumelhart's model shares assumptions with Sperling's (importance of the visual store and use of parallel scanning) but is more specific about the process by which pattern recognition occurs.

    2. Rumelhart believed that performance on the whole-report task was due to perceptual rather than memory limitations.

    3. Argued that recognition occurs by identification of features.

        a. Processing is parallel.

        b. Feature identification takes time.

    4. According to Rumelhart, performance in the visual report task is a function of both the clarity of the information and the number of items in the display.

        a. When display terminates, clarity declines as VIS contents decay.

        b. Number of items affects performance because limited attention is shared among all elements in display.

    5. Estes and Taylor's (1966) detection paradigm provides evidence for Rumelhart's model.

III. **Word Recognition**
  A. **Word Superiority Effect**
    1. Subjects can recognize a letter in a word faster than they can recognize the letter when it's presented either alone or in a nonword (Gerald Reicher, 1969).
    2. An example of top-down processing
    3. Explanation based on the *interactive activation model* (McClelland and Rumelhart, 1981). See Figure 2.13, p. 41. Assumptions:
      a. Visual perception involves parallel processing. 2 parallel processes -- 1) spatially parallel identification of letters, i.e., processing all four letters simultaneously (both Rumelhart and Sperling proposed parallel processing of information in visual display), and 2) recognition occurs at three levels of abstraction simultaneously (feature, letter, and word levels).
      b. Levels interact to determine what we see. Certain features, e.g., curves, limit possible letters to be considered.
      c. 2 kinds of connections between levels: excitatory (positive evidence) and inhibitory (negative evidence).
  B. **Neural Network (Parallel Distributed Processing) Models**
    1. Nodes (features, letters, words, etc.)
    2. Connections between nodes (excitatory or inhibitory)
    3. Activation rules (how nodes combine inhibitory and excitatory inputs with current state of activation)
    4. State of activation
    5. Output functions (relate the activation levels to outputs)
    6. Learning rules (how to change weights of connections)

CHAPTER 2: PRACTICE QUESTIONS (Answers and page references are on p. 166.)

Multiple Choice Questions: For each question, circle the single, best alternative.

1. Which theory states that we divide patterns into their parts and identify the parts in order to decide what the pattern is?

   a. template theory
   b. feature theory
   c. structural theory
   d. all of the above

2. According to Gibson's feature theory, features should remain unchanged under changes in

   a. brightness.
   b. size.
   c. perspective.
   d. all of the above

3. Sperling proposed that people use the visual information store (VIS) to preserve information for less than one second. The VIS is a

   a. sensory store.
   b. scan component.
   c. short-term memory process.
   d. long-term memory process.

14

4. Separating perceptual limitations from memory limitations was the reason the

    a. partial-report technique was invented by Sperling.
    b. whole-report technique was invented by Sperling.
    c. partial-report technique was invented by Rumelhart.
    d. whole-report technique was invented by Rumelhart.

5. The finding that it is easier to recognize a letter in a word than in isolation or in a nonword is called

    a. the "letter superiority effect."
    b. the "letter recognition effect."
    c. the "meaningful feature effect."
    d. the "word superiority effect."

6. Template theory states that

    a. we compare patterns with one another and measure how much they overlap.
    b. we divide patterns into features and test to see if they have the same features.
    c. we determine whether features have the same relations in two patterns.
    d. we know two patterns are the same when they have the same name.

7. The difference between intersection ($\cap$) and union ($\cup$) symbols can be explained by

    a. template theories of pattern recognition.
    b. feature theories of pattern recognition.
    c. structural theories of pattern recognition.
    d. all of the above

8. Structural theories of pattern recognition

extend feature theories by

a. including additional features.
b. including holistic analysis.
c. including specification of relations.
d. including nodes and connections.

9. The features that best determine similarity among the letters *N, C, P, F, R, E, M,* and *G* are

a. curved vs. straight.
b. vertical vs. horizontal.
c. horizontal vs. diagonal.
d. vertical vs. curved.

10. Errors in letter identification are best predicted by the

a. template model.
b. Gibson feature model.
c. Geyer and De Wald feature model.
d. Both feature models predicted better than the template model.

11. A geon conveys information about

a. features.
b. volumes.
c. preserved complementarity.
d. divided complementarity.

12. Sperling argues that inability to report more than 4 items accurately after a brief exposure is due to

    a. a memory limitation caused by decay from the VIS.
    b. a perceptual limitation caused by decay from the AIS.
    c. a partial report limitation caused by decay from the AIS.
    d. both *a* and *b*

13. The idea that small samples of behavior (e.g., tryouts) will generalize to larger samples (e.g., performance during the season) is the reasoning behind the

    a. partial-report paradigm.
    b. whole-report paradigm.
    c. word superiority effect.
    d. letter confusion effect.

14. Sperling proposed the visual information store to explain the ____ in the number of items correctly reported as the interval before the signal tone _____
_____.

    a. increase; increased
    b. increase; decreased
    c. decline; increased
    d. decline; decreased

15. A stimulus can be "erased" from the visual sensory store by

    a. visual intensity.
    b. visual duration.
    c. visual contrast.
    d. visual masking.

16. Rumelhart argues that inability to report more than 4 items accurately after a brief exposure is due to

    a. a memory limitation affected by the number and clarity of items in a display.
    b. a perceptual limitation affected by the number and clarity of items in a display.
    c. a partial report limitation inversely related to the clarity of items in a display.
    d. both *a* and *c*

17. Interaction of the feature, letter, and word levels of the interactive activation model offers a good explanation of the

    a. word superiority effect.
    b. visual masking effect.
    c. partial report effect.
    d. serial processing effect.

18. The interactive activation model states that the activation level of a letter depends on

    a. excitatory influences.
    b. inhibitory influences.
    c. both excitatory and inhibitory influences.
    e. neither excitatory nor inhibitory influences.

19. We are conscious of nodes that are

    a. connected to other nodes.
    b. disconnected from other nodes.
    c. activated above a threshold.
    d. activated just below threshold.

20. NET-TALK required 40,000 learning trials to learn to

    a. read as well as a 2-year-old.
    b. produce as many words as a 2-year-old.
    c. read as well as a college graduate.
    d. produce as many words as a college graduate.

21. The overlapping triangles figure (Figure 2.4) supports which theory?

    a. template theory
    b. feature theory
    c. structural theory
    d. all of the above

22. What does Donald Hoffman mean by "creative genius"?

    a. ability to use a tachistoscope
    b. ability to recognize patterns
    c. ability to test Sperling's model
    d. the word superiority effect

23. What is the most famous characteristic of a Necker cube?

    a. that it has more than 3 dimensions
    b. that it has fewer than 3 dimensions
    c. that the left and right sides appear to "flip-flop"
    d. that the back and front planes appear to "flip-flop"

24. Biederman's Component Model is used to describe what kinds of objects?

    a. 2-dimensional
    b. 3-dimensional
    c. geons
    d. nongeons

25. Letters are identified faster when they are in words than when they are not. What kind of processing is this an example of?

    a. Bottom-up
    b. geon
    c. template
    d. top-down

True-False Questions:

T F 1. Structural theories deny the existence of features.

T F 2. The intensity, contrast, and duration of a stimulus all affect decay from the visual information store (VIS).

T F 3. Information in the VIS is available for no more than 2.5 msec. before it decays.

T F 4. Rumelhart was the first to propose a visual sensory information store.

T F 5. When intersecting lines are deleted at their vertices, the recognition of objects becomes more difficult.

T F 6. The auditory information store (AIS) is a part of short-term memory.

T F   7.   Inhibitory feedback prevents one from recognizing the letter *K* when it appears in a field on its own (e.g., - - *K* -) as quickly as when it appears as part of a word (e.g., *WAKE*).

T F   8.   Neural network models are theories of parallel distributed processing.

T F   9.   Tachistoscopes are used to increase the probability of an experimental participant making an incorrect pattern identification.

T F   10.   In Phillip's experiment, experimental participants had to report whether the pattern of randomly filled cells had moved.

T F   11.   If you were an Irish Setter, you would distinguish better between Irish Setters than between Irish Wolfhounds.

Essay Questions:

1. Explain Sperling's and Rumelhart's interpretations of the partial report data. How do they differ?

2. Use the word superiority effect as a model and explain why an expert chess player might be able to identify a chess piece faster when it is embedded in a meaningful mid-game position than when it is alone on the board.

CHAPTER 3: ATTENTION

I. Attention: Selectivity and Concentration

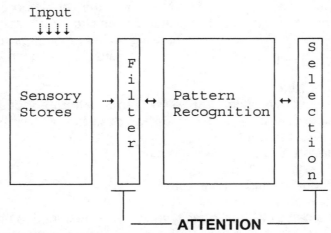

A. Filter and/or Selection
B. Bottleneck and Capacity Theories

II. Bottleneck Theories
A. Broadbent's Filter Theory
    1. Selection is based on sensory channels.
    2. Channels are defined by the physical characteristics of the stimuli.
    3. Mechanical model
        a. Only one channel at a time reaches pattern recognition stage.
        b. Switching channels requires both time and effort.
B. Treisman's Attenuation Model
    1. Simultaneous <u>meaningful</u> messages
    2. Experimental participants "shadowed" one ear and ignored other.
    3. Meaning was swapped between ears.
        a. Majority of subjects followed meaning.
        b. Information from the unattended ear <u>must</u> have been recognized.
    4. Treisman proposed that the filter is an *attenuation device* and <u>not</u> an "all-or-none" barrier.
        a. Selective filter
        b. "Dictionary"
        c. Recognition occurs if intensity is above word's threshold.

C. Deutsch-Norman Memory Selection Model
1. Places the bottleneck after pattern recognition
2. The bottleneck occurs during *selection*.
3. Model assumes that
   a. <u>All</u> incoming stimuli are recognized.
   b. Stimuli are quickly forgotten unless they are important and therefore selected for further processing for permanent storage.
   c. Selection for further processing based on both pertinence (importance) and the amount of sensory activation.

III. Capacity Theories
A. Assume that two tasks can be performed simultaneously <u>unless</u> the combination requires more attention than the system has available (*mental effort* is the key)
1. Allocation of capacity is affected by
   a. arousal
   b. enduring dispositions
   c. momentary intentions
2. Kahneman's (1973) Capacity model was designed to add to rather than replace the bottleneck theories.

B. Capacity and Stage of Selection
1. Johnston and Heinz's (1978) "multimode" theory of attention
   a. Effect of performing a primary task on the performance of a subsidiary task
   b. The degree to which tasks interfere with one another depends on how much processing must take place before selection can be performed.
2. Pashler's (1998) general model

IV. Automatic Processing
A. A skill is automatic if it ...
1. Occurs without intention
2. Does not give rise to conscious awareness
3. Does not interfere with other mental activities
4. Example: *Stroop Effect*

B. Automatic Encoding (*Incidental Learning*)
1. Kinds of information that might be automatically encoded
   a. Frequency information
   b. Spatial information
   c. Temporal information
2. If automatic, nothing should interfere with acquisition of such knowledge.
3. Substantial evidence that frequency information is automatically encoded. Evidence is mixed for spatial and temporal information.

C. Automatic Processing and Reading: LaBerge and Samuels' (1974) Letter Matching task
1. Time to make "match" vs. "no match" judgments for unfamiliar "letters" decreased with increased practice.
2. Practice does not affect time to make judgments for familiar letters.

D. Cell Phone Use
1. Divided attention
2. Accidents increase when cell phones are used.
3. Does not matter whether cell phone is a hand-held or "hands-free" device
4. Listening to the radio does NOT produce similar results.

CHAPTER 3: PRACTICE QUESTIONS (Answers and page references are on p. 167.)

Multiple Choice Questions: For each question, circle the single, best alternative.

1. Because attention does not have to be switched from ear-to-ear

   a. Broadbent's filter model predicts that it will be easier to report messages by attentional channel than by temporal order.
   b. Broadbent's filter model predicts that it will be easier to report messages by temporal order than by attentional channel.
   c. Triesman's attenuation model predicts that it will be easier to recognize your own name.
   d. Triesman's attenuation model predicts that shadowing will improve recognition of "unattended" items.

2. The finding that people could report information to the unattended ear in a shadowing task presented a problem for the

   a. selection model.
   b. attenuation model.
   c. filter model.
   d. capacity model.

3. In the Deutsch/Norman memory selection model the bottleneck occurs

   a. during sensory processing.
   b. before the pattern recognition stage.
   c. during the pattern recognition stage.
   d. after the pattern recognition stage.

4. The finding that more capacity is required for a late mode of selection supports _____ of attention.

   a. Broadbent's Filter model
   b. Triesman's Attenuation model
   c. Johnston and Heinz's Multi-mode theory
   d. Deutsch/Norman's Memory Selection model

5. Which model proposes that performance is limited by the mental effort tasks require?

   a. a bottleneck model
   b. a capacity model
   c. both models
   d. neither model

6. In Kahneman's Capacity model of attention, voluntary attention is controlled by

   a. subliminal perception.
   b. momentary intentions.
   c. enduring dispositions.
   d. evolutionary factors.

7. Which of the following is an adaptive response to information overload?

   a. spending less time on each input
   b. disregarding low-priority inputs
   c. completely blocking some sensory inputs
   d. all of the above

8. Pattern recognition is a major focus of _____ theories of attention.

   a. bottleneck
   b. capacity
   c. automatic processing
   d. information processing

9. The filter model was proposed to account for the fact that performance is worse

   a. with longer intervals between pairs.
   b. with shorter intervals between pairs.
   c. with the "shadowed" message.
   d. with the "un-shadowed" message.

10. When subjects respond to the contextual effects of language, they shift attention

    a. from one auditory channel to the other.
    b. from one visual channel to the other.
    c. from the "shadowed" to the "un-shadowed" ear.
    d. from the "un-shadowed" to the "shadowed" ear.

11. According to Anne Treisman, a word's threshold

    a. determines whether a word is recognized.
    b. is the maximum intensity required for awareness of activation.
    c. is higher for important than for unimportant words.
    d. all of the above

12. Attenuation of a visual stimulus would cause it to appear to be _____ than an un-attenuated visual stimulus.

    a. softer
    b. louder
    c. dimmer
    d. brighter

13. An example of an attentional model that states that all patterns are recognized before they're chosen for further processing is

    a. Broadbent's Filter model.
    b. Triesman's Attenuation model.
    c. Johnston and Heinz's Multi-mode model.
    d. the Deutsch-Norman Memory Selection model.

14. Is it true that the amount of mental effort required to perform a task depends only on the task?

    a. Yes, because it requires the same effort every time.
    b. No, because it doesn't require the same effort every time.
    c. No, because everyone's brain works the same way.
    d. Yes, because not everyone's brain works the same way.

15. Clanging alarms are effective because _____ will cause you to attend to them.

    a. allocation of capacity
    b. enduring dispositions
    c. momentary intentions
    d. sensory overload

16. Long reaction times to a subsidiary task in a selective listening experiment would indicate that

    a. the primary task did not require much attentional capacity.
    b. the primary task required a lot of attentional capacity.
    c. the subsidiary task was compatible with the primary task.
    d. both *a* and *c*

17. Time to respond to a light signal was longer when there were _____ than when there were _____

    a. no lists; two lists that could be distinguished using sensory cues.
    b. no lists; two lists that could be distinguished using semantic cues.
    c. two lists that could be distinguished using semantic cues; two lists that could be distinguished using sensory cues.
    d. two lists that could be distinguished using sensory cues; two lists that could be distinguished using semantic cues.

18. Most of the empirical support for Hasher and Zacks' theory of automatic encoding involves

    a. spatial information.
    b. frequency information.
    c. temporal information.
    d. intentional learning.

19. _____ is the reason that people are more likely to fail to identify a letter when it is part of a common word than when it is part of an uncommon word.

    a. Lack of intelligence
    b. Intelligence
    c. Unitization
    d. Unfamiliarity

20. Unrelated noncolor cues do not affect performance on a colored target but unrelated colored cues do. What does this imply about the relation of automatic and nonautomatic processes?

    a. They're different.
    b. They're the same.
    c. They interact.
    d. They don't interact.

21. Why does cell phone usage impair driving performance?

   a. Because the driver's hands are occupied.
   b. Because the driver's attention is divided.
   c. Because dialing requires that driver remove his/her hands from the steering wheel.
   d. None of the above.

22. The evidence for automatic encoding of spatial and temporal informal is mixed. This had led some researchers to the belief that these processes are not automatic. What other explanation is there?

   a. They are automatic and the experiments were flawed.
   b. They are automatic but the participants were not normal.
   c. They would become automatic if the participants practiced.
   d. There is no other explanation.

STUDY GUIDE FOR REED'S COGNITION
CHAPTER 3: ATTENTION

True-False Questions:

T F   1.   Bottleneck and capacity theories of attention share the same basic assumptions.

T F   2.   If the capacity required for performing a task is moderate, the task is performed automatically.

T F   3.   Broadbent's filter model places the attentional bottleneck before pattern recognition.

T F   4.   Treisman's attenuation model proposes an "all or none" attentional filter.

T F   5.   Shadowing is used to make certain the experimental participants don't attend to the shadowed message.

T F   6.   Because selection occurs after pattern recognition, only important inputs are recognized.

T F   7.   If two actions each require an amount of effort equal to a person's capacity, the two actions cannot be performed simultaneously.

T F   8.   The multi-mode theory of attention states that time to respond to a subsidiary task is a function of variations in primary task processing requirements.

T F   9.   The Stroop Effect is evidence that automatic processing is advantageous.

T F   10.   Tests of selective listening are poor predictors of ability to succeed in flight school.

T F   11.   Attention can be distributed flexibly.

Essay Questions:

1. In what way do capacity theories serve as an addition to the bottleneck theories of attention? Is there something that the bottleneck theories were lacking?

2. Pick a specific activity that you believe that you perform automatically. Using three of Hasher and Zacks' (1979) five criteria for determining automaticity, propose three ways to test this belief.

CHAPTER 4: SHORT-TERM WORKING MEMORY

I. **Forgetting**
   A. **Rate of Forgetting**
      1. Peterson and Peterson (1959) established that information in STM is lost rapidly *unless* it is rehearsed.
      2. Experimental design:
         a. 3 consonants presented
         b. 3 digit number presented
         c. Count backward by 3's from number until light appears (3, 6, 9, 12, 15, or 18 sec. later).
         d. Recall digits.
      3. Recall decreases as the delay increases
   B. **Cause of Forgetting: Decay vs Interference**
      1. *Decay Theory* = forgetting is spontaneous (would forget no matter what)
      2. *Interference Theory* = forgetting is due to trying to remember something else (using STM for another purpose)
      3. Waugh and Norman's (1965) *digit probe task* suggests that interference and not decay explains forgetting from STM.
      4. Experimental Design:
         a. Present 16 single digit numbers.
         b. Last digit in list is "probe" and it occurred exactly once earlier in list.
         c. Subject is to respond with the digit that came after probe in list, e.g., for string "3 4 6 5 7 3 2 9 1 6 8 9" (the probe = "9", and the correct answer is "1").
         d. Position of probe in list was varied (1 to 12 intervening items).
         e. Rate of presentation was varied (1 or 4 digits/sec).
      5. Results:
         a. Rate of presentation has no effect.
         b. More intervening items = poorer recall
   C. **Wickens (1963) *Release from Proactive Interference* study showed that semantically similar materials cause more interference than dissimilar materials do.** (Peterson and Peterson's subjects did not show forgetting on early trials.)
      1. Experimental Design:
         a. 3 numbers or 3 common words presented.
         b. 20 sec. delay (filled with a task to prevent rehearsal)
         c. 4 trials (12 items total)

       i.   Control group = all 4 trials were items from same semantic class
      ii.   Experimental group = first 3 trials from same class, last trial from a different class (if words then numbers or vice versa)

  2. Results:
     a. Control group shows less recall on each subsequent trial.
     b. Experimental group performance declines from Trial 1 to 3, but then Trial 4 recall = Trial 1 recall.
  3. Similar results were obtained by Gunter, Clifford and Berry (1980) using more complicated materials such as sports reports on the news.

II. Capacity
A. The Magic Number 7
  1. *Absolute Judgment* studies: identifying stimuli that vary along a single, sensory continuum
  2. *Memory Span* studies: number of items that can be recalled immediately after a serial presentation
  3. George Miller's paper is so famous because:
     a. it drew attention to how little upper limit varies in absolute judgment and memory span tasks.
     b. it contributed the idea of *chunking* (recoding information) to overcome limitations of STM.

B. Individual Differences in Chunking
  1. De Groot (1966) asked chess players to reproduce a mid-game board. Experts reproduced 90% while weaker players only reproduced 40%.
  2. Chase and Simon (1973) measured time between successive pieces (longer than 2 sec. pauses = chunk boundary). Experts have more chunks (7.7 vs 5.3 for beginners), and their chunks are larger (2.5 vs 1.9 pieces)
  3. Simon and Gilmartin (1973) estimated that expert chess players have 10,000 to 100,000 chunks stored in memory.

III. Memory Codes
A. Acoustic Codes and Rehearsal
  1. Relation between memory span and rehearsal
     a. Faster pronunciation is associated with larger memory span.
     b. Faster retrieval is associated with larger memory span.
     c. Pronunciation and retrieval speeds are unrelated.
  2. *Acoustic confusions*
     a. Errors <u>sound</u> like correct response
     b. *Phonemes* account for errors

    c. Laughery's model assumes that each acoustic component can be forgotten separately

   3. Acoustic codes in reading

    a. *Subvocalizing* facilitates detailed recall

    b. Changes in read text were:

      i. Semantic -- words were the same, meaning was changed

      ii. Lexical -- word was changed, meaning was retained

    c. Subvocalizing doesn't affect recognition of main ideas when paraphrasing alters them

IV. Recognition of Items in STM

A. Searching STM [Paradigm invented by Saul Sternberg (1966)]

   1. *Memory set* is memorized

   2. Test digit is presented

   3. Is test digit a member of memory set?

   4. Results:

    a. With each additional item added to the target set, RT increased by approx. 38 msec

    b. RTs for positive and negative responses were about the same

    c. No effect on reaction times of location of test item in target set

   5. Conclusion: Search is serial and exhaustive

B. Degraded patterns

   1. Two operations required to determine whether a test item is in the memory set

    a. Encoding — determining identity of test item

    b. Scanning — checking to see if identity matches an item in memory set

   2. Intercept (reaction time required to scan a memory set with no items in it) is a function of encoding process.

   3. Slope (increase in reaction time for each item added to the memory set) is a function of scanning process.

   4. Results support conclusion that degraded stimuli only affect encoding process.

V. Working Memory
A. Baddeley's Working Memory Model
1. Three Components:
   a. *Phonological Loop* (maintains and manipulates acoustic information)
   b. *Visuospatial Scratch Pad* (maintains and manipulates visual/spatial information)
   c. *Central Executive* (responsible for managing the working memory system)

CENTRAL EXECUTIVE CONTROL SYSTEM
(Central Pool of mental resources)
<u>Activities</u>:
Initiate control and decision processes
Reasoning, language comprehension
Transfer information to LTM via rehearsal, recoding
Recency Effects

PHONOLOGICAL LOOP
(Short-Term Buffer)
<u>Activities</u>
Articulatory processes, e.g., verbal rehearsal
Recycling items for immediate recall
Executive's resources are drained if articulatory task is difficult

VISUOSPATIAL "SCRATCHPAD"
<u>Activities</u>
Visual imagery tasks
Executive's resources are drained if imagery task is difficult

---

2. Baddeley has experimented with preventing the use of the various components to see how they affect performance.
   a. Experimental Design: Dual-task paradigm: De Groot's chess board reproduction task + a simultaneous second task
      i. To prevent use of Phonological loop, 2nd task = repeating a string of digits (e.g., 1 2 3 4 5 6)
      ii. To prevent use of Scratchpad, 2nd task = tap a series of keys in a predetermined pattern
      iii. To prevent use of Central Processor, 2nd task = repeating a string of <u>random</u> letters (e.g., Z N T F)
   b. Results:

        i. Interfering with Visuospatial Scratchpad and/or Central Processor reduces memory for chess pieces.

        ii. Interfering with Phonological Loop does not.

B. Working Memory vs. STM

1. STM is a component of working memory
2. Short-tem memory is separate from the central executive.
   a. The central executive's primary function is controlled attention.
      i. maintain task goals
      ii. scheduling
      iii. maintain task information
      iv. suppress irrelevant information
   b. STM maintains activated memory traces.

C. Baddeley's Revised Working Memory Model

1. How can different memory codes be brought together?
2. fourth component of model: episodic buffer
   a. storage system that can integrate memory from different modalities
   b. creates multimodal code to represent the environment
3. LTM is included (to account for interaction of working memory with LTM)

CHAPTER 4: PRACTICE QUESTIONS (Answers and page references are on p. 168.)

Multiple Choice Questions: For each question, circle the single, best alternative.

1. Compared to novices, chess experts have

   a. better memory for the positions of pieces on a chess board, but only if the pieces are arranged in a fashion that respects the rules of chess.
   b. better memory for the positions of pieces on a chessboard, no matter how the pieces are arranged.
   c. better visual memories in general.
   d. no memory advantage.

2. Use of the visuospatial scratchpad for a primary task can be prevented by having subjects

   a. say "A, X, R, M, D, F" over and over.
   b. tap a series of keys in a predetermined pattern.
   c. count from 1 to 10 repeatedly.
   d. Any of the above will work.

3. Asked to recall a series of individual words, a subject makes a sentence using all of the words. The subject is placing the to-be-recalled words into a memory unit known as a(n)

   a. chunk.
   b. image.
   c. package.
   d. sentence.

4. In Language A, all numerals have one-syllable names. In Language B, all numerals have two- or three-syllable names. We would expect speakers of Language A to have _____ than speakers of Language B.

   a. a smaller number of memory chunks
   b. a slightly larger digit span
   c. less effective rehearsal strategies
   d. fewer phonological confusions

5. Information cannot be retained in STM longer than _ unless it is rehearsed.

   a. 180 msec
   b. 1.8 sec
   c. 18 sec
   d. 180 sec

6. Which of the following is indicative of acoustic confusions?

   a. Errors that look like the correct response.
   b. Errors that have the same meaning as the correct response.
   c. Errors that sound like the correct response.
   d. all of the above

7. Sternberg demonstrated that scanning does not occur before encoding, by showing that

   a. degraded stimuli do not alter the slope of the function relating RTs to the size of the memory set.
   b. degraded stimuli alter the slope of the function relating RTs to the size of the memory set.
   c. the size of the memory set does not affect the time required to respond "yes, a probe item is in the memory set."
   d. the size of the memory set affects the time required to respond "yes, a probe item is in the memory set."

8. Three times in succession, I give you names of five countries to recall. On the fourth trial, I give you the names of five fruits to recall. The pattern of your recall attempts will demonstrate

   a. proactive interference.
   b. retroactive interference.
   c. release from proactive interference.
   d. release from retroactive interference.

9. In proactive interference,

    a. information in STM interferes with information in LTM.
    b. information in the sensory store interferes with information in LTM.
    c. previously presented information interferes with subsequent learning.
    d. recently learned information interferes with prior learning.

10. In Cowan's study, students with fast pronunciation rates

    a. also had fast retrieval rates.
    b. had smaller memory spans.
    c. had larger memory spans.
    d. *a* and *c*

11. The difference between the following two sentences is an example of a _____ alteration.

    The kindly lady helped the sick child.
    The kindly woman helped the sick child.

    a. lexical
    b. syntactic
    c. semantic
    d. paraphrase

12. George Miller is famous for

    a. formulating the concept of working memory.
    b. showing the relation between processing time and capacity of short-term memory.
    c. identifying the capacity of short-term memory.
    d. showing that chess masters have larger memory chunks than do novices.

13. When acoustic confusions occur, the error most likely involves

    a. a word with a similar meaning.
    b. a word with an opposite meaning.
    c. a letter that sounds similar.
    d. a letter that sounds dissimilar.

14. Laughery argues that acoustic confusions occur because a word's

    a. phonemes are all forgotten.
    b. phonemes are forgotten independently.
    c. meaning is remembered but the exact word is not.
    d. meaning is not clearly understood.

15. If subvocalization is suppressed during reading, students will have the easiest time identifying changes involving

    a. lexical alterations.
    b. paraphrasing.
    c. semantic alterations.
    d. All of the above are equally easy to identify.

16. Sternberg's "memory set"

    a. was stored in STM at the beginning of each trial.
    b. was stored in LTM at the beginning of each trial.
    c. was visually available during each trial.
    d. was acoustically available during each trial.

17. The phonological loop has two components. They are

    a. visual and acoustic stores.
    b. lexical and semantic stores.
    c. a phonological store and a rehearsal mechanism.
    d. a phonological store and a comparison mechanism.

18. Which of the following is not a function of the central executive?

    a. maintaining task goals
    b. maintaining activated memory traces
    c. suppressing task irrelevant information
    d. planning sequences of actions

19. Chess performance is a function of the actions of the

    a. central executive.
    b. phonological loop.
    c. visuospatial scratchpad.
    d. both a and c.

20. Why is it easier to remember a proverb than a unfamiliar sentence of the same length?

    a. chunking due to familiarity
    b. proactive release due to familiarity
    c. phonological rehearsal is easier
    d. the visuospatial scratchpad can be used

21. What component did Baddeley add to his model to allow memory codes represented in different modalities to interact?

    a. central executive
    b. episodic buffer
    c. phonological loop
    d. visuospatial scratchpad

22. What component of memory plays the biggest role in recall of highly familiar scenes?

    a. episodic buffer
    b. long-term memory
    c. phonological loop
    d. visuospatial scratchpad

True-False Questions:

T F   1.   Forgetting from STM occurs even when nothing interferes with the stored information.

T F   2.   Waugh and Norman's probe digit task showed that presentation rate affects recall of the test digit.

T F   3.   You have to study for three classes that have very different course content. To maximize the amount you will remember, you should study each for a short time and then switch (as opposed to completing one class's material before you begin on the next).

T F   4.   Absolute judgment tasks require one to decide whether/how one stimulus compares to another (e.g., louder).

T F   5.   One of the characteristics of expertise is the ability to create large chunks that organize meaningless information.

T F   6.   Acoustic codes are created while reading by using subvocalization.

T F   7.   The slope of the line relating RT to memory set size can be used to determine the speed with which a test digit is compared to the items in the memory set.

T F   8.   Baddeley's revised memory model is likely to generate research into the role of the sensory stores in working memory.

T F   9.   The phonological loop is an important component of chess skill.

T F   10.   "Working memory" and "short-term memory" are two different phrases that describe the same thing (they are synonymous).

Essay Questions:

1. Explain why Sternberg concluded that degrading an item only affects the encoding and not the scanning process, when scanning the contents of STM.

2. Use the following sentence and create (a) a lexical alteration, (b) a semantic alteration, and (c) a paraphrase.

   The President of the United States vetoed a bill sent to him by the Congress.

CHAPTER 5: LONG-TERM MEMORY

I. **Atkinson-Shiffrin Model (1968, 1971)**
  A. **Three basic *control processes*** can be used to move information from STM to LTM.
    1. *Rehearsal* is the repetition of information over and over until it is learned.
    2. *Coding* is a way of placing new information in the context of easily accessible, old information. Two common coding techniques include mnemonics (e.g., the word HOMES gives the first letter of the names of the Great Lakes) and categorization (e.g., a Manx is a kind of cat).
    3. *Imaging* is a way of creating visual images to remember verbal information. Imaging techniques include the Method of Loci and other visualization tricks.
  B. **Verbal rehearsal and Learning**
    1. Verbal rehearsal is a form of *rote learning*.
      a. Students are given paired associates to learn (e.g., 28-L). They are shown each to-be-learned pair for 3 sec., with a 3 sec. blank interval between each pair.
      b. Test items consisting of only the two-digit numbers were interspersed and the students had to name the letter that had been paired with the number.
      c. One of the independent variables in the experiment was the number of trials between study and testing of a pair. Some pairs were tested on the very next trial (0 delay) while others weren't tested until 17 additional pairs had been studied.
    2. A fixed number of items is held in STM. Model assumes that rehearsal of items in STM occurs whenever the person is not otherwise occupied.
    3. Rehearsal transfers items from STM to LTM.
    4. Learning is, therefore, a function of both rehearsal and the number of intervening items.
      a. More rehearsal = more learning
      b. More intervening items (greater delay) = less recall
  C. **Rehearsal and the Serial Position Effect**
    1. *Serial Position Effect* (U-shaped curve that results when recall is plotted against position in the to-be-learned list). See line with round points in Fig. 5.2, p. 102.

2. Better recall of the items from the beginning of the list is called the *Primacy Effect* (caused by retrieving from LTM items that were rehearsed "extra" times).

3. Better recall of the items from the end of the list is called the *Recency Effect* (caused by retrieving from STM items not yet processed/rehearsed <u>or</u> items from LTM that are more distinctive because of their position at the end of the list).

II. Control Processes

A. How memory is used to learn information. Among the decisions to be made are:

1. Acquisition strategies:
   a. Processing choices: rehearsal, imaging, coding?
   b. How to allocate study time?
2. How can the information be maintained?
3. What retrieval strategies will be useful if it's hard to recall the information?

B. Judgments of Learning (JOLs): Dunlosky and Nelson (1994) had students learn half of a set of paired associates using an imagery strategy and half using a rehearsal strategy.

1. The imagery strategy was more effective than the rehearsal strategy (respectively, 59% vs. 25% correct recall).
2. Students were more accurate at identifying which strategy was superior when they made delayed judgments (30 sec. after studying a pair) than when they made immediate judgments.
3. Delayed judgment of learning also produced more accurate determinations of whether individual pairs had been learned.
4. *Retrieval Fluency* is a poor indicator of learning because it is often a result of reporting the contents of STM.

C. Allocation of Study Time

1. Atkinson compared the learning of 84 English translations of German words for students who either chose which words they wanted to study or who had the words chosen for them by a computer program that used a learning model to determine which words should be studied.
2. The students who had words selected for them on the basis of the learning model learned many more translations than students who selected for themselves which words to study.

D. Retrieval Strategies

1. Preliminary search of LTM to determine whether there is relevant information in LTM -- if there is, one must determine how to conduct search.
2. *Tip-of-the-tongue* (TOT) phenomenon occurs when you know that you know something BUT you can't recall it at the moment.
   a. Partial information, e.g., first initial or length of word, helps to limits search of LTM.
   b. Laboratory studies produce TOT by giving definitions or descriptions to students and asking for the name of the object or person.
   c. Naturalistic studies ask people to keep a diary and record TOT states as they occur.
   d. Both types of studies show that recall of partial spelling information is the predominant retrieval strategy. More *spontaneous retrievals* occurred when the TOT state occurred naturally than when it was produced in the laboratory.

III. Improving Eyewitness Recall and Identification
A. Improving Eyewitness Recall

1. Although hypnosis increases recall, it may increase inaccurate recall or may result from either the repeated testing or reinstatement of the context (neither of which is hypnosis-specific).
2. Geiselman, Fisher, MacKinnon and Holland (1985) tested three interview conditions:
   a. Standard Interview (normal law-enforcement procedures).
   b. Hypnosis Interview (subjects were hypnotized prior to being asked to recall)
   c. Cognitive Interview (subjects were encouraged to reinstate the context, report everything, recall events in different orders and from different perspectives)
3. Both hypnosis and the cognitive interview produced more recall than the standard interview. Cognitive interview is <u>most effective</u> because it is easier to learn and administer than the hypnosis interview.
4. U. S. Department of Justice based its guidelines for collecting eyewitness testimony on this and other related experiments.

B. Eyewitness Identification

1. In 36 of 40 wrongful convictions, mistaken eyewitness testimony was implicated (Wells et al., 2000).
2. Biasing effects of mug shots can be due to confusion about context in which person was seen.

   a. Viewing mug shots significantly increased likelihood of identifying a person as having committed a crime regardless of their guilt.
   b. False identifications occur because familiarity is increased as a result of exposure to the photograph.
   3. Investigators may bias identifications by tone of voice or body language.

IV. Indirect vs. Direct tests of Memory

   A. Direct tests of memory, e.g., recognition and/or recall tests, make reference to a particular event in a person's past.
   B. Indirect tests of memory, e.g., word completion or word identification, refer only to the current task and do not refer to prior events.
   C. Direct and Indirect tests can yield different information regarding memory for an item.
   1. Warrington and Weiskrantz (1970) have shown that amnesiac subjects perform as well as nonamnesiacs on word-fragment (identify a degraded word) and initial-letter tests (complete a word given the first three letters).
   2. The same amnesiacs performed worse than the nonamnesiacs on recall and recognition tests covering the same material.
   D. Explanations:
   1. Different processing requirements
       a. Direct tests require both a judgment of familiarity and an attempt to retrieve context in which information was originally presented.
       b. Indirect tests require only familiarity judgment.
       c. Experiments by Jacoby and Dallas (1981) demonstrated that changing familiarity of item (via manipulation of context at learning and test) affects performance on both recognition memory and perceptual identification tasks. In contrast, manipulating variables which affect identification of context in which items were encountered (generation via anagram vs. read only) only affected performance on the recognition memory task.
       d. Performance on direct tests is conceptually driven, e.g., top-down. Performance on indirect tests is data-driven, e.g., bottom-up.
   2. Different memory systems: *Semantic, episodic, and procedural*
       a. Direct tests require episodic memory.
       b. Indirect tests require semantic or procedural memory.
   3. Brain Structures -- Damage to the hippocampal formation in the medial temporal lobe causes explicit memory performance problems for amnesiacs

CHAPTER 5: PRACTICE QUESTIONS (Answers and page references are on p. 169.)

Multiple Choice Questions: For each question, circle the single, best alternative.

1. The "primacy effect" refers to

   a. increased recall for the items at the beginning of a list relative to items in the middle of the list.
   b. decreased recall for the items at the beginning of a list relative to items in the middle of the list.
   c. increased recall for the items at the end of a list relative to items in the middle of the list.
   d. decreased recall for the items at the end of a list relative to items in the middle of the list.

2. If a student recalls only 12 words from a list of 25 words, the unrecalled words will most likely come from the

   a. beginning of the list.
   b. middle of the list.
   c. end of the list.
   d. both *a* and *c*

3. If you just finished memorizing the names of all of the U.S. Presidents in chronological order when a sudden loud noise distracted you for 2 minutes, this would depress memory for

   a. the earliest Presidents.
   b. the "middle" Presidents.
   c. the most recent Presidents.
   d. all of the Presidents equally.

4. Which of the following is not an example of a recognition test?

   a. Is the person that you said was a good speaker in the group over there?
   b. If I show you a list of names, will you be able to tell me who was at the meeting?
   c. What's an eight-letter word for "work out" that begins with "E"?
   d. Is this how you spell "parallel": P A R A L L E L?

5. Dunlosky and Nelson found that delayed judgments of learning were <u>inferior</u> to immediate judgments when judging

   a. which of two learning strategies was most effective.
   b. which individual items were learned.
   c. both of the above
   d. neither of the above

6. The following list is presented: *garden, house, tree, yard, driveway, staircase, rooms, windows.* Immediately after the list is presented, John is asked to recall it. He remembers *windows, rooms, garden.* and *house.* John's recall is an example of the

   a. primacy effect.
   b. recency effect.
   c. serial position effect.
   d. proactive interference effect.

7. An effective way of making sure that you will remember something a long time from now is

   a. to repeat it over and over to yourself.
   b. to shut out all distractions when you're studying.
   c. to review the material at regular intervals.
   d. to learn the material really well right now and then not worry about it until later.

8. Which of the following is not an acquisition strategy proposed by Atkinson and Shiffrin?

   a. coding
   b. imagery
   c. learning
   d. rehearsal

9. Rote learning uses

   a. elaboration.
   b. imaging.
   c. mnemonics.
   d. repetition.

10. Rundus's data show that percent recalled

    a. is a function of number of rehearsals for items in the beginning and middle of long lists.
    b. is an inverse function of number of rehearsals for items in the beginning and middle of long lists.
    c. is a function of number of rehearsals for items at the end of long lists.
    d. both *a* and *c*

11. Immediate judgments of learning are _____ accurate than delayed judgments because the information is in __.

    a. less; STM
    b. more; STM
    c. less; LTM
    d. more; LTM

12. A poor indicator of which items will be recalled after a delay is

    a. the primacy effect.
    b. retrieval fluency.
    c. storage fluency.
    d. spaced retrieval.

13. Which of the following will produce more tip-of-the-tongue episodes?

    a. giving definitions of common words
    b. giving definitions of unfamiliar words
    c. giving definitions of unusual words
    d. *a, b,* and *c* should produce an equal number of episodes

14. The best way to improve eyewitness identification is to use

    a. standard police questioning.
    b. hypnosis.
    c. a cognitive interview.
    d. rehearsal.

15. Mug shots can bias eyewitness testimony. This is because

    a. the degree of familiarity can be assessed.
    b. the degree of familiarity cannot be assessed.
    c. the context of familiarity can be distinguished.
    d. the context of familiarity cannot be distinguished.

16. Testing to see whether a previously provided set of definitions affects the subject-produced definition of a word with two meanings (a homograph) when no reference is made to the previous set of definitions is an example of

    a. a recognition test of memory.
    b. a direct test of memory.
    c. an indirect test of memory.
    d. a judgment of learning.

17. Expanding upon and categorizing information are examples of

    a. recognition processes.
    b. data-driven processes.
    c. conceptually-driven processes.
    d. procedural memory processes.

18. The term "multiple memories" used in distinguishing between indirect and direct memory tests refers to

    a. recognition and recall memories.
    b. episodic, procedural, and semantic memories.
    c. spontaneous memory retrievals.
    d. rote and elaborative memories.

19. Learning can be represented as the transfer of information from

    a. sensory memory to short-term memory.
    b. short-term memory to sensory memory.
    c. short-term memory to long-term memory.
    d. long-term memory to short-term memory.

20. Information decays from long-term memory

    a. faster than from sensory memory.
    b. faster than from short-term memory.
    c. more slowly than from short-term memory.
    d. more slowly for rehearsed than for elaborated items.

21. How does time pressure affect study time allocation?

    a. High pressure leads to more study of easy items.
    b. High pressure leads to more study of hard items.
    c. Low pressure leads to greater study of hard items.
    d. Time pressure doesn't affect allocation of study time.

22. What effect does the retrieval of related words have on eventual recall of target items?

    a. They always are helpful.
    b. They always are harmful.
    c. They are sometimes helpful.
    d. They have no effect.

23. Which biasing effect do experts feel most comfortable about testifying about in court when asked to testify about the accuracy of eyewitness testimony?

    a. accuracy/confidence confound
    b. hypnosis
    c. long-term repression
    d. wording of questions

24. Which biasing effect do experts think that the general public is most likely to misevaluate?

    a. accuracy/confidence confound
    b. hypnosis
    c. long-term repression
    d. wording of questions

25. Why shouldn't the administrator of a line-up know which person in the line-up is the suspect? It might introduce bias due to

    a. body language.
    b. confidence.
    c. false alarms.
    d. mug shots.

True-False Questions:

T F   1.   Word length can be used to search long-term memory for a word
            that is known but is currently un-retrievable.

T F   2.   In the long run, names and concepts are equally easy to
            remember.

T F   3.   The best way to move an item from short-term memory to long
            term memory is to rehearse it.

T F   4.   Eyewitness identification is more reliable if only one mug shot has
            been shown to the eyewitness.

T F   5.   Tip-of-the-tongue episodes demonstrate that information can be
            permanently lost from LTM.

T F   6.   The inverted "U" produced by the serial position effect shows that
            recall is worst for items at the beginning and end of long lists.

T F   7.   People are better at choosing words to study than a learning
            model is because people know themselves best.

T F   8.   Delayed judgments of learning are more accurate than immediate
            judgments of learning because they rely on short-term memory.

T F   9.   A major concern related to the use of hypnosis in eliciting
            eyewitness testimony is the possibility that it will increase the
            number of incorrect facts that are "retrieved."

T F   10. Damage to the hippocampal formation in the medial temporal lobe
            causes poor performance on indirect memory tests.

Essay Questions:

1. Why is retrieval fluency at immediate recall related to the failure to observe a negative recency effect when recall of a serially-presented list is delayed?

2. What are some of the factors that can bias eyewitness testimony? Given that there are so many things that can affect the accuracy of such testimony, why do you think the legal system allows eyewitnesses to testify?

CHAPTER 6: MEMORY CODES

I. **Levels-of-Processing Theory (Craik and Lockhart, 1972)**
   A. **Emphasis on Coding Strategies** -- If STM and LTM were truly different memory stores with different characteristics, the distinctions between STM and LTM should have been clearer.
   B. **Different ways to code the same material**
      1. Sensory processing (preliminary/shallow processing)
      2. Pattern recognition (intermediate level of processing)
      3. Semantic-associative processing (deep processing)
   C. **Different codes have different decay rates**
      1. Sensory-only processing results in fast decays.
      2. If patterns are recognized and named, then intermediate decay results.
      3. Processing of meaning produces the best memory (slowest decay).
   D. **Levels-of-processing theory extends stage model of memory by showing how control processes affect retention of material.**

II. **Supporting Evidence for the Levels-of-Processing Approach to Memory**
   A. **Hyde & Jenkins (1969)** *Incidental Learning* **Experiment**
      1. Read a list of 24 words.
         a. 12 pairs of *primary associates* (e.g., red-green) randomly ordered
         b. No pair of related words presented together
      2. 4 groups (really 7) compared on variety of incidental learning tasks
         a. Try to remember.
         b. Has an 'e'?
         c. Pleasant?
         d. How many letters?
      3. Free recall results:
         a. 'try' = 16.1 (16/24 = 2/3)
         b. 'e' = 9.4 (9/24 = a little more than 1/3)
         c. 'pleasant?' = 16.3
         d. number of letters = 9.9.
      4. "Pleasant group" attended to meaning of words, as did "try to learn group", the other two groups did not.
         a. Clustering (pairing of semantically related words at recall) was 26% for 'e', 31% for number of letters, and a whopping 64% for 'try to learn' and 68% for "pleasant?"
         b. Meaning aided recall of last two groups.

B. Structural, Phonemic and Semantic Processing (Craik and Tulving, 1975)
1. Three conditions varied type of processing engaged in:
   a. *Structural* = "capitals?"
   b. *Phonemic* = "rhyme?"
   c. *Semantic* = "fit in sentence?"
2. Results:
   a. Recall increases with increases in depth of processing
   b. "Yes" responses result in greater recall than "No" responses

III. Criticisms and Modifications of the Theory
A. Criticisms
1. Too easy to account for differential forgetting rates -- Would have to be able to measure depth independently of recall to address this criticism
2. Even if "depths" are known, doesn't explain why some are better than others

B. Elaboration of Memory Codes
1. Anderson & Reder (1979) say that memory codes differ in the number and type of elaborations stored in memory.
2. Craik and Tulving (1975) results showed that "yes" responses produced better recall for all levels of analysis than "no" responses.
3. Idea is that you store not only the to-be-remembered information but that you also store associations with those items.
4. Elaboration is more easily accomplished at the semantic level than at the syntactic or phonemic levels, but in principle, elaboration can occur at any level of analysis.
5. Craik and Tulving (1975) showed that elaboration, if appropriate, does affect recall even if all material is analyzed to semantic level.
   a. They increased semantic elaboration by increasing the complexity of sentences subjects had to determine whether a target word fit into.
   b. 3 levels of complexity for the word "chair": simple, medium, complex, e.g.,
   Simple: She sat in the _____.
   Medium: The antique _____ was uncomfortable.
   Complex: The skilled carpenter constructed the _____ without using any nails.
   c. 60 judgments about whether word fit in sentence
   d. Recall (cued followed by noncued) as many of 60 words as possible.

    e. Sentence complexity had significant effect on recall of words <u>that fit sentences</u>.
       i. For words that fit sentences, more complex sentences led to better recall.
       ii. For words that didn't fit sentences, sentence complexity is irrelevant to recall.
    f. Elaboration must be consistent with to-be-remembered word.
       i. Precise vs. imprecise elaboration
       ii. Imprecise elaboration produced worse recall than that of the control group.

C. Distinctiveness of Memory Codes
    1. Memory codes can differ in *distinctiveness* as well as in elaborateness.
       a. *Distinctiveness* refers to the distinguishability/separability of one item from another.
       b. Four kinds of distinctiveness:
          i. *Primary distinctiveness* is relative to immediate context.
          ii. *Secondary distinctiveness* is defined relative to information in LTM.
          iii. *Emotional distinctiveness* is defined by the production of strong emotions.
          iv. *Processing distinctiveness* is defined in terms of how the stimulus was processed.
    2. For elaboration to be truly effective, it should emphasize characteristics that make one item different from others.

IV. Encoding Specificity and Retrieval
  A. Encoding Specificity Principle
    1. Some retrieval cues are better than others.
       a. Memory traces differ in the kinds of information they contain.
       b. Even if encoding is held constant, differences in recall occur.
       c. Encoding and retrieval interact (must match for best recall).
    2. Mood-dependent memory is an example.
  B. Interaction between Encoding and Retrieval Operations
    1. Thompson and Tulving's (1970) demonstration that recall can exceed recognition
       a. Students were asked to memorize paired associates in which the cue words were only weakly associated with the target words, e.g., *country OPEN*.
       b. Next they were given a list of words which are strongly associated with the original target words, e.g., *shut* (a close associate of

"open") and asked to write down the first four words they thought of for each of the strongly associated cues.

   c. Then they were asked to circle all of the associates they had generated which had appeared as targets on the original list.

      i. In other words, each of them created his/her own recognition test.

      ii. Recognition was poor.

      iii. The change in context/elaboration failed to serve as an effective cue for accessing the stored information.

   d. Last, the subjects were provided with the original cues/weak associates and asked to recall the original TARGET words.

      i. Recall was excellent.

      ii. Reinstating the initial context/elaboration made recall better than recognition.

  2. Light and Carter-Sobell's (1970) recognition experiment

   a. Adjective-noun pairs were capitalized in sentences, e.g., The TREE had dappled BARK.

   b. Recognition test required subjects to determine whether a noun had been on the sentence list.

   c. At test, the nouns were presented alone, with the same adjective or with a different adjective (e.g., dog bark).

   d. Recognition was best with the same adjective and worst with the different adjective.

  3. Fisher and Craik's (1977) study of the effect of similarity between encoding context and retrieval cue was directed toward answering the question -- does deeper encoding always result in better memory?

   a. Subjects were given an incidental learning task that emphasized either semantic or phonemic encoding of words.

   b. At retrieval, subjects were either presented with the identical context in which they had encountered the word earlier, e.g., "Associated with boot?" or "Rhymes with blue?;" a similar context, e.g., "Associated with sandal?" or "Rhymes with grew?;" or a different context, i.e., phonemic if semantic originally or vice-versa.

   c. On average, recall in the identical context was greater than recall in the similar context which, in turn, was greater than recall in the different context.

V. Transfer-appropriate processing

  A. A general consequence of the encoding specificity principle is that the value of specific learning strategies depends on the nature of the goal.

B. **Student performance is affected by the type of test studied for (multiple choice vs. essay).**

C. **Fact- vs. problem-oriented acquisition of knowledge affects performance on problem solving tasks.**

D. **How are transfer-appropriate processing and encoding specificity related?**

    1. similar in that both rely on the "match" between encoding and retrieval operations

    2. different in that the matching either occurs at encoding (transfer-appropriate processing) or retrieval (encoding specificity)

CHAPTER 6: PRACTICE QUESTIONS (Answers and page references are on p. 170.)

Multiple Choice Questions: For each question, circle the single, best alternative.

1. Remembering information about a stimulus in addition to what you intended to remember (e.g., position on a page) is called

   a. accidental learning.
   b. elaborative learning.
   c. incidental learning.
   d. intentional learning.

2. The fact that subjects often remember some aspect of the context in which a word is learned and store it as part of the memory trace is an example of

   a. background learning.
   b. encoding specificity.
   c. implicit memory.
   d. multiple encoding.

3. If a subject paid attention to the sounds of the words when trying to memorize a list, which of the following questions will be easiest to answer?

   a. Was there a word that was printed in capital letters on the list?
   b. Was there a word that rhymed with "tree" on the list?
   c. Was there a word that had the same meaning as "ship" on the list?
   d. Was there a word on the list that could be used to complete "___ light?"

4. Which kind of distinctiveness is determined by the relation of an item to LTM?

   a. primary distinctiveness
   b. secondary distinctiveness
   c. emotional distinctiveness
   d. processing distinctiveness

5. A subject who memorized the pair "spelling-bee" from a list later denied that any of the words "honey," "bee," "hive," or "buzz" was on the original list. This is most likely because

   a. the learning context does not provide adequate support for perceptual encoding.
   b. the learning context does relatively little to encourage deep processing.
   c. what was memorized was the idea of "bee" as an event, not "biological creature."
   d. the learning context encouraged thinking of compound words, while the test context encouraged thinking of semantic associates.

6. Which of the following strategies will produce the most learning? Determining whether

   a. there are more vowels or consonants in a word.
   b. a word is a noun or a verb.
   c. a word has more than two syllables.
   d. a word rhymes with "nevermore."

7. Studying with no intention to memorize the material, but with the intention to understand how the concepts are related will result in

   a. poor learning, because no attempt was made to memorize the concepts.
   b. poor learning, because shallow processing is used to study.
   c. good learning, because shallow processing is used to study.
   d. good learning, because deep processing is used to study.

8. Consider the way in which elaboration affects recall. Which of the following sentences should provide the best retrieval cue for "elated"?

   a. The elated woman answered the phone.
   b. The elated woman won a cellular phone.
   c. The elated woman received a phone call from her mother.
   d. The elated woman used her cellular phone to call her mother.

9. Elaboration is difficult at which level of processing?

   a. structural
   b. phonemic
   c. semantic
   d. both *a* and *b*

10. The finding that students generally do better on an exam when the format (multiple choice, essay) matches their expectations is an example of

    a. elaboration.
    b. transfer-appropriate processing.
    c. levels-of-processing.
    d. distinctiveness.

11. Suppose you are presented with the phrase *calorie free* and are asked to recall it later. Which of the following is the best retrieval cue?

    a. born free
    b. caffeine free
    c. free enterprise
    d. free will

12. According to the levels-of-processing model proposed by Craik and Lockhart, the coding of an item

    a. determines whether an item is in STM or LTM.
    b. determines the speed with which the item will be forgotten.
    c. is determined by the number of rehearsals.
    d. is determined by the intrinsic nature of the item.

13. Craik and Lockhart (1972) proposed the levels of processing model because

    a. there were clear distinctions between the characteristics of STM and LTM.
    b. there were not clear distinctions between the characteristics of STM and LTM.
    c. Rundus demonstrated that recall is a function of the length of time an item is held in STM.
    d. the elaboration and distinctiveness of memory codes do not affect recall.

14. A major criticism of the levels of processing model is

    a. that it provides no *a priori* reasons for specifying the "depth" of a particular kind of processing.
    b. that it offers no explanation of why some codes are more effective than others.
    c. that it is too easy to account for differential forgetting rates by appealing to the theory.
    d. all of the above.

15. Which retrieval cue for the word "Flower" should be least effective if the question in an orienting task was "Rhymes with Tower"?

    a. a kind of plant
    b. rhymes with Bower
    c. rhymes with Tower
    d. none, since all should be equally effective

16. Being unable to recall why you started dating your partner when you're in the middle of a fight is an example of

    a. autobiographical memory.
    b. emotional memory.
    c. mood dependent memory.
    d. flashbulb memory.

17. Orienting tasks are used to

    a. make sure people know what's going to happen next.
    b. control the processing strategies people use.
    c. ensure that people try to memorize the stimuli.
    d. all of the above

18. What would be the strongest (best) evidence for separate long- and short-term memory systems?

    a. single, slow decay rate for STM and single, fast LTM decay rate
    b. single, fast decay rate for STM and single, slow LTM decay rate
    c. multiple decay rates for STM and single, fast LTM decay rate
    d. multiple decay rates for LTM and single, fast STM decay rate

19. The fact that bilinguals tend to recall events from their lives that correspond to the language they are speaking is an example of what?

    a. distinctiveness
    b. elaborative processing
    c. encoding specificity
    d. transfer-appropriate processing

20. How do encoding specificity and transfer-appropriate processing differ?

    a. in match between encoding and retrieval
    b. in timing of the encoding/retrieval match
    c. one relies on STM and one on LTM
    d. one use phonemic codes and the other semantic codes

True-False Questions:

T F 1. A memory code is the representation used to store an item in memory.

T F 2. The longest-lasting memory codes result from the use of maintenance rehearsal.

T F 3. Incidental learning tasks are used to control the kind of processing a person applies to an item.

T F 4. Memory codes based on semantic processing produce the most retrieval.

T F 5. In an incidental learning experiment, subjects are told that they should try to remember the materials.

T F 6. Clustering in recall occurs when people fail to notice that to-be-remembered information is interrelated.

T F 7. Processing meaning without intent to memorize produces recall as good as intentional memorization.

T F 8. Semantic processing occurs when you count the number of vowels in a word.

T F 9. Emotional memories are more accurate than ordinary memories.

T F 10. Orthographic distinctiveness refers to the shapes of words.

Essay Questions:

1. Why do you think the majority of people are unable to predict the relative effectiveness of retrieval cues?

2. Suppose a friend tells you that even though she studies hard, she can't seem to remember anything when she's taking a test. She says the problem doesn't have anything to with "test anxiety." Based on what you learned from this chapter, suggest two possible explanations of your friend's test performance.

CHAPTER 7: VISUAL IMAGES

I. **Visual Imagery and Learning**
   A. **Memory for Pictures**
      1. Shepard (1967) showed that recognition of 612 pictures was as good after a week (87%) as recognition of 612 words was immediately after learning (88%).
      2. Standing (1973) also showed that recognition of pictures is excellent (6,600 of 10,000).
         a. Other groups saw 1,000 words, 1,000 ordinary pictures, or 1,000 unusual pictures.
         b. 615 words, 770 ordinary pictures, and 880 unusual pictures were correctly recognized.
   B **Paivio's Dual Coding Theory**
      1. *Concrete/Abstract* (Paivio, 1969) dimension is primary determinant of recall.
         a. *Imagery potential* (how easy is it to form an image?)
         b. *Association value* (how many associates can be generated in 1 min.)
         c. Imagery potential is a better predictor of learning than is association value.
      2. Dual-Coding explanation of better recall for pictures than words
         a. Paivio (1971) has long argued that LTM uses both verbal and visual codes to represent information.
         b. View has come to be known as the *"Dual-coding theory."*
         c. Visual and verbal information are represented <u>and</u> processed in functionally independent cognitive systems.
            i. One system, the visual system, is assumed to be specialized for processing information concerning concrete objects and events.
            ii. The other system, the verbal system, is specialized for dealing with language kinds of information (1975).
         d. A possible explanation of the superiority of memory for pictures over that for verbal material may be that, with two (possible) codes for a single stimulus, there <u>may be twice as many access routes to the information.</u>
         e. Paivio conducted a number of experiments to try to support his dual-coding viewpoint.
            i. Most of these were directed toward demonstrating that pictures and concrete words (*high imagery potential*) are learned better than abstract words (Paivio, 1971).

        ii. Or that when both verbal and imaginal codes are utilized, retention is better than when only one is involved (Paivio, 1978).
    f. Criticism is that dual coding only works when people focus on *relational information*.

C. Comparison of Association Learning Strategies
    1. Bower and Winzenz's (1970) Learning Strategies experiment
        a. All subjects memorized pairs of *concrete* nouns.
        b. Four conditions:
            i. Repetition
            ii. Sentence reading
            iii. Sentence generation
            iv. Image generation
        c. Results:
            i. *Recognition* was high in all four conditions.
            ii. *Recall* was worst for the repetition group and best for the imagery group.

D. The Mnemonic *Keyword* Method and Vocabulary Learning
    1. Form an association between the spoken foreign word and an English word that sounds approximately like it.
    2. The English word is called the "keyword," and it must be a word that has an easily imaginable concrete meaning.
    3. Create a mental image in which the keyword and the English translation are interacting in some fashion.
    4. Investigators have found enormous improvements in memory for paired associates when imagery is used in this way.
        a. In one study (Atkinson and Raugh, 1975) imagery subjects scored over 70% correct while control subjects scored only 46% correct.
        b. The imagery technique has been shown to improve recall by as much as 100 to 150% over ordinary learning methods.

II. Evidence for Images in Performing Cognitive Tasks:
    A. Scanning Visual Images -- Kosslyn and Pomerantz (1977) provided evidence that images were spatial representations (albeit internal to the subject) that had the same properties as "real" (i.e., nonimaginal) pictures.
    1. Demonstrated that subjects used the same operators to perform scanning tasks on both real and imagined stimuli.
    2. Subjects memorized locations of seven (7) items on a map. (See Figure 7.4, p. 164.)
    3. Real map removed.

4. Told to imagine map, focus on named object, imagine speck moving in straight line to location of second named object.
5. Press button upon arrival at second location.
6. There are 21 distances among the 7 locations. Largest distance is 9 times the shortest distance.
7. For real pictures, scanning time is a linear function of real distance.
   a. Results showed that *imaginal* scanning is linearly related to real distances.
   b. Presumably distances between imagined locations are linearly related to real distances.
8. Criticism: Maybe subjects are just trying to please the experimenter, and RTs reflect not scanning time but expected time to perform task.
   a. Mitchell & Richmond (1980) showed that subjects could accurately predict the effect of distance on scanning time.
   b. Reed, Hock, and Lockhart (1983) showed that people cannot accurately predict the effect of pattern shape on scanning time (e.g., spiral vs. straight line). At same time showed that length of line to be scanned was linearly associated with scanning time.

B. Sequential vs. Parallel Processing -- Neilsen and Smith (1973) gave students either verbal descriptions or pictures of people.
   1. Each face had five features (ears, eyebrows, eyes, nose, mouth).
   2. Neilsen and Smith varied the number of relevant features (3, 4, or 5).
   3. After study period (4 sec), shown a picture and asked whether it matched earlier description or picture
   4. Results: Number of relevant features only affects face to description comparison <u>not</u> face-to-face comparison.
   5. Similar to Sternberg's STM scanning results

C. Mental Transformations
   1. Shepard and Metzler's (1971) mental rotation experiment
      a. Subjects looked at pairs of figures constructed to have special properties.
         i. *"A" pairs* were identical except that one member of the pair had been rotated on the plane defined by the surface of the page.
         ii. *"B" pairs* were identical except that one member of the pair had been rotated on the plane perpendicular to the surface of the page (rotated through the third dimension, back into the page).
         iii. *"C" pairs* were not identical. The two figures looked similar, but it was impossible to rotate one so that it was identical to the other.
      b. A, B, and C pairs were presented to subjects at various angles.

        c. The task was to say whether the two members of the pairs were "identical" (A and B pairs) or "different" (C pairs).

            i. Shepard and Metzler hypothesized that if mental images have the characteristics of real world objects, then, if the two images are misaligned, the subjects would have to "mentally rotate" one figure into the other in order to determine whether they were identical.

            ii. A prediction Shepard and Metzler derived from their theory that mental images have the characteristics of real objects is that the greater the angle of rotation, the longer it should take subjects to determine whether the two objects were identical.

        d. Time to respond "identical" or "different" was the dependent variable used in the study.

        e. The results showed that, when the angle of rotation was very small (close to 0°), subjects took an average of one second to respond; however for a 180° rotation they took about 4.5 seconds on average.

    2. Mental Animation

        a. Students evaluated static and kinematic statements about a diagram.

        b. Location of pulleys had no effect on the evaluation of static statements.

        c. Location of pulleys did affect RTs for the evaluation of kinematic statements (later in sequence = longer RT).

D. Interference

    1. Evidence for separate visual and verbal systems has been produced by Brooks (1968).

    2. Brooks demonstrated that shifting between visual and verbal material can reduce interference.

    3. Brooks assumed that if there are separate verbal and visual systems then it should be possible to selectively interfere with performance by varying whether the responses are given visually or verbally.

        a. A verbal response requires an overt yes/no response. Verbal responding, if there really are separate systems, should interfere more with the sentence (verbal) task than with the $\mathbb{F}$ (visual) task.

        b. Conversely, visual responding (point to a Y for each yes response or a N for each no response) should interfere more with the visual than with the verbal task.

    4. Four groups:

        a. Visual task/Visual response

        b. Visual task/Verbal response

        c. Verbal task/Verbal response

       d. Verbal task/Visual response
- 5. Time to complete each task was DV.
- 6. Results showed that selective interference was indeed occurring. If the response was in the same modality as the task, responses were slower than if the responses were given in the other modality.
- 7. Sanders and Schroots (1969) have shown that memory span can be increased if to-be-stored items come from different modalities (e.g. spatial vs. verbal).

E. Evidence from Cognitive Neuroscience
- 1. Cerebral blood flow and ERPs show activity in visual cortex for visual imagery task but not for mental arithmetic or memory scanning task
- 2. Persons with brain damage show the same preserved and impaired functions for both visual imagery and vision, e.g., *visual neglect*

III. Limitations of Images
A. Memory for Details
- 1. Nickerson and Adams (1979)
  - a. Showed that most people *cannot* select correct representation of a penny from a set of 15 possible pennies.
  - b. Visual memory is selective (only important features are encoded).
- 2. Chambers and Reisberg's (1992) duck/rabbit experiment
  - a. Showed that people had trouble re-interpreting a *mental image* (as a duck or a rabbit) because they selectively maintained only the more important features (the "face" part of their interpreted image).
  - b. They had no trouble re-interpreting the original picture.

B. Reality monitoring
- 1. People with good imagery abilities have trouble distinguishing between seeing and imagining (Johnson and Raye, 1981).
- 2. Possible cues:
  - a. Sensory information
  - b. Contextual information
  - c. Cognitive operations

C. Breakdown of reality monitoring
- 1. Long delays between incident and recall
- 2. Repeated suggestions that event occurred
- 3. Perceived authority of source of suggestions
- 4. Perceived plausibility of suggestions
- 5. Mental rehearsal
- 6. Use of hypnosis or use of guided imagery

CHAPTER 7: PRACTICE QUESTIONS (Answers and page references are on p. 171.)

Multiple Choice Questions: For each question, circle the single, best alternative.

1. Studies of image scanning indicate that

    a. subjects' scanning rate is slow for short distances but is faster for greater distances.
    b. there is a linear function linking scanning distances and scanning times.
    c. fastest scanning times tend to be obtained with moderate scanning distances.
    d. subjects are able to scan across their image virtually instantaneously.

2. A subject is shown a map of Paris. On the map, Notre Dame and the Eiffel Tower are 2.5 inches apart; Notre Dame and the Arc de Triomphe are 5 inches apart. The subject is instructed to form a mental image of the map and scan the distance from Notre Dame to the Arc de Triomphe. It takes the subject 3 seconds to do so. How long should it take the subject to scan from Notre Dame to the Eiffel Tower?

    a. 1.5 seconds
    b. 2.0 seconds
    c. 2.5 seconds
    d. 3.0 seconds

3. According to Paivio, it is easier to memorize words if they

    a. are abstract.
    b. invoke images.
    c. have high association value.
    d. have low association value.

4. According to the results of imagery experiments, which of the paired associates shown below should be the easiest to learn?

   a. cognition-interest
   b. teacher-apple
   c. picture-ability
   d. strain-table

5. According to the results of imagery experiments, which of the paired associates shown below should be the hardest to learn?

   a. cognition-interest
   b. teacher-apple
   c. picture-ability
   d. strain-table

6. Brooks found that people could better perform a memory task by verbally responding rather than pointing to answers on an answer sheet when the task was

   a. classifying the corners of a block diagram.
   b. classifying the words in a sentence.
   c. both of the above
   d. neither of the above

7. Which of the following is not a characteristic of a good keyword for learning foreign vocabulary words?

   a. Sounds like the foreign word or some part of the foreign word
   b. Is similar to the other keywords
   c. Can easily form an interactive image with the English translation
   d. Is easily imaginable

8. Of which of the following is the forming of visual images an example?

   a. rote rehearsal
   b. semantic elaboration
   c. elaborative processing
   d. all of the above

9. That visual and verbal memory codes are independent is a main assumption of

   a. Watson's theory of behavioral imagery.
   b. Lutz and Lutz's theory of interactive imagery.
   c. Paivio's dual-coding theory of memory.
   d. Pylyshyn's theory of propositional memory.

10. The concrete/abstract dimension is

    a. only relevant for studies of verbal learning.
    b. an important determinant of imagery potential.
    c. an important determinant of association value.
    d. not a good predictor of learning.

11. When people cannot predict the outcome of a scanning experiment

    a. their scanning times cannot be trusted.
    b. evidence for the use of a linear slope in mental scanning is more convincing.
    c. evidence for the use of propositional codes in mental scanning is more convincing.
    d. evidence for the use of imagery in mental scanning is more convincing.

12. The correct order of recall (best to worst) for word pairs that differ in imagery potential (H = High Imagery potential, L = low) is

    a. L-L > H-L > L-H > H-H.
    b. L-L > L-H > H-L > H-H.
    c. H-H > H-L > L-H > L-L.
    d. H-H > L-H > H-L > L-L.

13. Which of the following cues help you to distinguish reality from imagination?

    a. sensory
    b. contextual
    c. cognitive operations
    d. all of the above

14. Repeated suggestions from an authority figure might induce someone to

    a. remember true details from childhood.
    b. remember false details from childhood.
    c. forget true details from childhood.
    d. forget false details from childhood.

15. Subjects can reinterpret visual images if they are

    a. encouraged to use the image's name during the retrieval process.
    b. discouraged from using the image's name during the retrieval process.
    c. encouraged to label the images during initial processing.
    d. discouraged from labeling the images during initial processing.

16. Kosslyn assumes that visual mental images _____ visual perception.

    a. are indistinguishable from
    b. share processing subsystems with
    c. do not share processing subsystems with
    d. are more detailed than the images resulting from

17. Activation of the visual cortex occurs during

    a. mental arithmetic tasks.
    b. memory scanning tasks.
    c. visual imagery tasks.
    d. all of the above

18. For which of the following sequences would memory span be largest?

    a. K θ H ρ o M π o F
    b. o θ π ρ o π π o o
    c. Q D R M X O T L G
    d. Because all of the sequences have 9 items, memory span should be the same for them all.

19. There were more verification errors for

    a. static statements about the beginning pulley.
    b. static statements about the end pulley.
    c. kinematic statements about the beginning pulley.
    d. kinematic statements about the end pulley.

20. A possible explanation for the inability to choose the correct drawing of a penny from a set of similar drawings is that

    a. busy people aren't detail-oriented.
    b. only some details are relevant in everyday situations.
    c. pennies aren't worth much and so people don't pay much attention to them.
    d. the subjects in the experiment were from another country and were not familiar with pennies.

True-False Questions:

T F   1. Watson's (1924) *Behaviorism* encouraged the study of visual imagery.

T F   2. That visual images can improve performance on many cognitive tasks is evidence that Pylyshyn's Propositional Theory is correct.

T F   3. Paivio argued that people can create either verbal or visual elaborations but not both.

T F   4. Mnemonic techniques are used to improve memory.

T F   5. Bower and Winzenz (1970) found that a sentence-generation condition produced more learning than sentence-reading or imagery conditions.

T F   6. Creating bizarre images is always more effective than creating plausible images when learning associations.

T F   7. Students in Atkinson and Raugh's Russian vocabulary experiment learned almost twice as many translations if they used keywords than did the control subjects.

T F   8. When subjects can accurately estimate the amount of time it will take to mentally scan a distance, their RTs are more easily interpreted than when they can't estimate correctly.

T F   9. Visual neglect of the left half of the stimulus field results from damage to the left parietal lobe.

T F   10. People find it more difficult to reinterpret visual images than line drawings.

Essay Questions:

1. Suppose that a friend is taking Organic Chemistry and has to learn the names and atomic weights of all of the organic elements, e.g., Carbon = 8. What advice would you give your friend about using imagery to help him/her memorize the pairs?

2. Are you convinced that the verbal and visual memory systems are independent? Explain.

CHAPTER 8: CATEGORIZATION

I. **Five Benefits of Forming Concepts (Bruner, Goodnow, Austin, 1956):**
   A. **Reduces complexity of the environment**
   B. **Identification**
   C. **Reduces need for constant learning**
   D. **Allows decisions re: appropriate actions**
   E. **Enables structuring of knowledge**

II. **Concept Identification**
   A. **Discovering Rules and Attributes**
      1. People solve concept identification problems by evaluating hypotheses
      2. Hypotheses are abandoned when they are contradicted and new hypotheses are generated that fit the known information
      3. Rule Learning (given relevant attributes, figure out the rule)
      4. Attribute Learning (given a logical rule, figure out the attributes)
   B. **Critique of the Concept Identification Paradigm**
      1. Artificially constructed categories consist of a small number of dimensions and a small number of attributes on each dimension.
      2. Category membership is perfectly defined by one of several logical rules.
      3. Thus, an exemplar could be classified unequivocally as either a member or nonmember of the artificial category.
      4. Eleanor Rosch and her colleagues -- 1970's
         a. Traditional concept formation research "missed the boat" in one especially critical way, having to do with the nature of the concepts people were expected to acquire in traditional experiments.
         b. Natural categories tend to be composed of continuous dimensions and are hierarchically organized.
         c. Natural categories are not composed of equally good members (some members are more representative of the category than others).

III. Natural Categories

A. The Hierarchical Arrangement of Categories.

1. The highest level of the hierarchy, *Superordinate categories*, like "furniture" and "vehicles" are the most general. (Category members have little in common.) These categories are largest.
2. The next level in the hierarchy is the *basic level*. (Category members share many features and have few features in common with members of other basic level categories.)
   a. Basic-level categories are most differentiated.
   b. They are the first learned, and the most used in language (single words).
   c. Object verification is fastest for basic-level labels, e.g., "Chair" except for experts in their area of expertise. In area of expertise, equally fast at verifying subordinate membership as basic membership.
   d. Objects in categories can be represented by *prototypes* (average of category members). Averaged pictures of basic-level category members are identifiable.
3. At the lowest level in the hierarchy are *subordinate categories*. (Category members share lots of features with one another and they also share lots of features with other subordinate categories.) These categories are smallest. For example, "living room chair" and "dining room chair" are subordinate categories.

B. Typicality and Family Resemblances

1. *Typicality* = how well a category member represents a category
   a. Typicality due to *Family Resemblance*
   b. More typical members have more in common with other members of category.
   c. Least typical have fewest attributes in common with other category members.
2. Not relevant to *goal-derived categories* (family resemblance does not predict "goodness" of membership, satisfaction of goal/ideal does)
3. Clinical diagnosis relies on these ideas about natural categories.
   a. Diagnostic categories are comprised of large sets of overlapping attributes -- patients are more or less typical of disorder.
   b. Encourages clinicians to expect diversity among patients with same diagnosis and to respond appropriately to individual differences.

C. Person Perception -- Stereotypes are the result of exaggerated within group similarity.

D. Loss of Categorical Knowledge

1. Selective loss of knowledge of *living vs. nonliving categories* appears to be a result of loss of *visual features vs. functional features.*
2. Damaging a neural network's visual features (0%, 20%, 40%, 60%, 80%, or 100%) affected ability to identify living things but not nonliving things.
3. Eliminating functional features reversed the above-described results.

IV. Categorizing Novel Patterns
A. Categorization Models
1. *Nearest-neighbor rule* = compare new stimulus to all members of relevant categories, assign to category containing most similar member. Disadvantage is that although the new stimulus is compared to all other category members, only one is used to make decision.
2. *Average-distance rule* = compare new stimulus to all members of relevant categories, compute similarity to each member of each category, sum similarities to each category, divide by number of comparisons, assign to category with highest average.
   a. Advantage = uses all category members as basis for decision
   b. Disadvantage = must compute average similarity as well as comparing novel stimulus to all category members
3. *Prototype rule* = For each category, create a mental representation of a *prototypical* ("best") member of the category and compute similarity between prototypes and novel stimulus. Assign to category that has the most similar prototype.
   a. Advantage = only a few comparisons are necessary
   b. Disadvantage = how to handle noncontinuous attributes, e.g., marital status?
4. *Feature-frequency rule* = Compare a novel stimulus to all members of relevant categories. Count how many features each category member and the novel stimulus have in common. Add up feature counts for each category and assign to category with highest feature count.
   a. Disadvantage = lots of calculations
   b. Advantage = no problem with discontinuous dimensions
5. Both the Nearest-neighbor model and the Average-distance model are examples of Exemplar models (categorization is based on comparison to category exemplars).
6. Reed's data suggest that a prototype model with weighted features best describes how people classify schematic faces.
B. Limitations of Prototypes
1. Feature-frequency model best predicts club membership when dimensions are not continuous (e.g., marital status).

2. Medin and Schaffer's (1978) model proposed that people store examples of category patterns in memory and classify new patterns by comparing them with retrieved examples. Unlike nearest neighbor and average distance models, this model uses combinations of features to measure similarity.
3. Early learning results are more consistent with a prototype model; later results are more consistent with an exemplar model.

C. Theory-based Categorizations
1. Using theories about real-world to make categorization decisions
2. In an experiment in which *age* was the best predictor of who lived in which suburb and *education* was the worst, 50% of the participants rated *income* as the most predictive information because of their real-world experience that people of similar incomes live together.
3. People tend to pay more attention to features that provide causal explanations for category membership.
4. It is easier to learn to classify objects that appear to be coherent (make sense given prior knowledge of the world) than objects that appear to be incoherent (don't make sense given what one knows about the world).

CHAPTER 8: PRACTICE QUESTIONS (Answers and page references are on p. 172.)

Multiple Choice Questions: For each question, circle the single, best alternative.

1. Farrah and McClelland found that their neural network model had difficulty identifying nonliving objects when it lost

    a. articulatory features.
    b. phonemic features.
    c. functional features.
    d. visual features.

2. Categories that are organized around ideals are

    a. subordinate categories.
    b. basic categories.
    c. superordinate categories.
    d. goal-derived categories.

3. How did Bruner and his colleagues believed that concept identification problems are solved?

    a. attribute learning
    b. rule learning
    c. hypothesis testing
    d. prototype analysis

4. According to prototype theory, the mental representation for each concept

    a. represents an average or ideal for the category's members.
    b. specifies the necessary and sufficient conditions for category membership.
    c. is a definition of the category's center.
    d. lists the perceptual features that are found only in that category.

5. Saying, "There is a family resemblance among all the members of the Jones family," means that

   a. at least one feature is shared by all the members of the family.
   b. there is at least one identifying feature such that if you have that feature, you are certain to be a member of the family.
   c. every pair of family members will have certain features in common even though there may be no features that all of the family members have.
   d. there are several features that all members of the family have in common.

6. Subjects are certain that tomatoes are fruits even though they're a poor example of a fruit. This indicates that judgments about category membership

   a. depend on a judgment of typicality.
   b. are not entirely settled by an assessment of typicality.
   c. are independent of typicality.
   d. do not conform to the requirements of a definition.

7. The term "basic-level category" refers to

   a. the level of categorization regarded by most subjects as indisputable.
   b. the most general level of categorization subjects can think of.
   c. the most specific level of categorization subjects can think of.
   d. the most natural level of categorization, neither too specific nor too general.

8. Family resemblance scores are not useful in predicting typicality for members of _____ categories.

   a. basic-level
   b. subordinate
   c. superordinate
   d. goal-derived

9. Which consequence of categorization was <u>not</u> mentioned by Bruner, Goodnow, and Austin? Categorization

   a. reduces the need for constant learning.
   b. enables us to order and classify events.
   c. increases the complexity of the environment.
   d. allows identification of objects in the world.

10. You are told the relevant attributes and asked to identify the logical rule that defines a category. Of what is this an example?

   a. attribute learning
   b. rule learning
   c. hypothesis testing
   d. prototype analysis

11. At which level in Rosch's taxonomy would the phrase *reading lamp* belong?

   a. subordinate level
   b. basic level
   c. superordinate level
   d. polyordinate level

12. Causality plays a large role in what kind of categorizations?

   a. attribute-based
   b. family resemblance-based
   c. prototype-based
   d. theory-based

13. Rapid classifications at the superordinate level are

   a. more common than rapid basic level classifications.
   b. common for experts in their area of expertise.
   c. likely for goal-oriented categories.
   d. none of the above

14. Superordinate and goal-derived category members

   a. have many features in common.
   b. have few features in common.
   c. have high family resemblance scores.
   d. can easily be used to create prototypes.

15. Which dimension would be the least difficult to represent in a prototype model?

   a. major in school
   b. grade point average
   c. preferred music style
   d. eye color

16. People are most likely to use prototypes in classification tasks when

    a. they have had a lot of training.
    b. they have had very little training.
    c. dimensions are continuous.
    d. experimenters tell them to do so.

17. Coherent exemplars are easier to categorize than incoherent exemplars. This provides support for which model of categorization?

    a. feature frequency
    b. nearest-neighbor
    c. prototype
    d. theory-based

18. An example of an exemplar model is the

    a. prototype model.
    b. nearest-neighbor model.
    c. feature frequency model.
    d. all of the above

19. Differences in how well members of a category represent the category are differences in

    a. level.
    b typicality.
    c. frequency.
    d. both *a* and *b*

20. Natural categories are hierarchical because

    a. some members are more typical than others.
    b. some members have higher family resemblance scores.
    c. some groups are subsets of others.
    d. both *a* and *b*

True-False Questions:

T F   1. Categorization allows us to decide what constitutes an appropriate action.

T F   2. Because they fit organized knowledge structures called *schemas*, some exemplars are considered to be coherent while others that don't fit are considered incoherent.

T F   3. Attribute learning involves being given the attributes and having to identify the rule that defines the concept.

T F   4. The concept of typicality can be applied to artificial category members.

T F   5. Basic category members have more in common than subordinate category members.

T F   6. It is easy to form prototypes of superordinate category members.

T F   7. Living and nonliving things are identified by both their visual and functional features.

T F   8. Novel patterns are always categorized by comparison to a prototype.

T F   9. The feature frequency model is an exemplar model.

T F   10. There is a single, best model to account for categorization behavior and it is the prototype model.

Essay Questions:

1. Explain why it is difficult to represent noncontinuous dimensions using a prototype model.

2. Define family resemblance and typicality. Explain the relation between them.

CHAPTER 9: SEMANTIC ORGANIZATION

I. **Hierarchical Organization**
    A. **Recall of Hierarchical Information:** Bower, Clark, Winzenz, & Lesgold's (1969) hierarchical organization experiment
        1. Subjects were given the same information about minerals, plants, body parts, and instruments presented either in *randomly organized* hierarchies or in *meaningful* hierarchies. One of the meaningful hierarchies is shown on p. 216 of the text.
        2. Students remembered substantially more of the information when it had been presented in a meaningfully organized hierarchy.
            a. Meaningful: they remembered 65% after first trial and 100% after three study trials
            b. Random: they remembered less than 65% even after four study trials
    B. **Category Size**
        1. Each category in hierarchy is subdivided into smaller categories.
        2. People spontaneously group information into categories that contain 2 to 5 pieces of information.
            a. Chase and Ericsson's (1979) subject chunked random digits into units of 3 to 4 digits each (that represented running times) and increased his digit span to 70 items.
            b. Broadbent (1975) had people recall categorized information (e.g., the names of the seven dwarfs) and found that recall chunks consisted of approximately 3 items.
            c. Detterman and Ramig (1978) found that the average number of sentences in a paragraph was 2 for newspapers, 3 for novels, and 5 for textbooks, and that the average sentence consisted of 2.4 parts.
    C. **Building Semantic Networks**
        1. Texas Christian University (Holley and Dansereau, 1984) has devoted a lot of effort to investigating learning/studying. One of their foci has been *semantic networks*.
            a. Networks are typically represented by diagrams in which concepts are called nodes and the lines showing relationship between two concepts are called links.
                i. Links can be labeled or not (if simple).

ii. Figure 9.3, p. 219 of the textbook shows a semantic network representing information in a nursing text about wounds. (Two kinds of hierarchical relations: *p* = part, *t* = type; and two nonhierarchical relations: *c* = characteristics, and *l* = leads to are represented.)

b. This chapter is organized as shown in the semantic network below

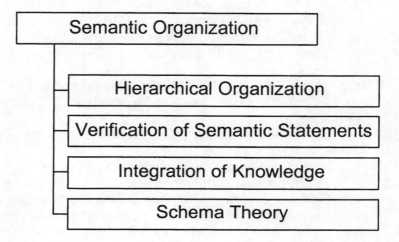

2. Students trained to construct semantic networks did significantly better than control subjects on essay and short-answer tests but performed similarly on multiple-choice tests.

II. The Standard Experimental Paradigm: Verification of Semantic Statements

A. The Paradigm

1. Experimenter presents statement and asks subjects to respond *true* or *false* as quickly as possible.
2. Time it takes to respond to different kinds of statements provides clue to semantic organization.
3. Hierarchical organization influences time to verify semantic statements.
4. Two common findings:
   a. People can generally verify that an instance is a member of a basic level category faster than they can verify that it is a member of a superordinate category.
   b. People classify more typical instances faster than less typical instances, e.g., "canary is a bird" is faster than "ostrich is a bird." Called the *Typicality effect*.

B. Hierarchical Network Model

1. Each concept is represented in the model by a node.
2. Each concept is stored with pointers -- the pointers are one-directional and show how it is related to other concepts in network.
3. Following pointers shows concepts that are related.
4. Features are stored at highest level at which they are true of all below. This is a form of cognitive economy.
5. Model assumes two things:
   a. Takes time to move from one level to another
   b. Takes <u>additional</u> time to retrieve features stored at one of the levels
6. Collins and Quillian (1969) had people respond true or false as quickly as they could to sentences like, "An elm is a plant" or "A spruce has branches."
   a. First sentence is a statement about set relations (is one category a member of another).
   b. Second sentence is a statement about properties (asks about features of a category member).
   c. Results are shown in Figure 9.6, p. 223 of the textbook.
      i. Response time depends on number of levels considered (supports idea that it takes time to move through network).
      ii. Longer to respond to property questions (supports idea that additional time is required to retrieve attributes/features of concept)
7. Another interesting prediction of hierarchical network concerns facilitating retrieval from memory. (Facilitation occurs when it is easier to retrieve some information because you just retrieved similar information.)
8. Two findings model does not account for:
   a. Instances in which verification time is not a function of levels in hierarchy.
      i. Model predicts verification time should be a function of number of levels.
      ii. Violations of *category size effect*
   b. The *typicality effect*

C. Feature Comparison Model (Smith, Shoben, and Rips, 1974)
1. This model attempts to explain the findings that the Collins and Quillian model fail to account for as well as explaining (albeit differently) those it does account for.
2. Model assumes that meaning of words is stored in memory as a list of features.
    a. Features can be used to define a category, <u>but</u>, they vary in extent to which they are associated with category.
    b. Smith, Shoben and Rips considered the most essential features to be *defining features* and the remainder to be *characteristic features*.
    c. Defining features are features an entity must have in order to be a member of a category.
    d. Characteristic features are usually possessed by category members but are not necessary.
3. Because defining features are more essential, they should play more important role in classifications.
4. Feature Comparison Model has two stages:

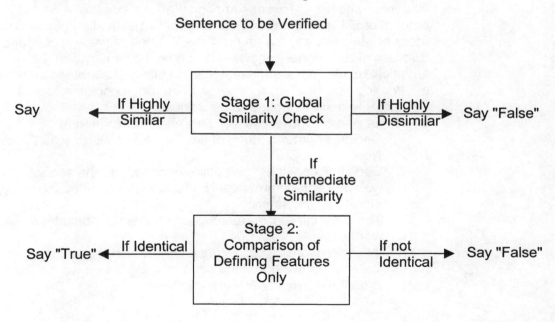

     5. Advantages over the Hierarchical Network Model:
       a. Ability to account for typicality effect
       b. Can account for reversal of category size effect
     6. Limitations of the Feature Comparison Model:
       a. Relies on ratings to make most of its predictions
       b. Proposal that all comparisons require computations
       c. Concept of necessary or defining features (think about Rosch and the characteristics of natural categories)

D. Spreading Activation Model
     1. Emphasis on concepts joined together by links that show relationships.
       a. Length of a link represents degree of relatedness of two concepts.
       b. See example in Figure 9.7, p. 228 of text
     2. Can account for the typicality effect
     3. Model assumes that when a concept is processed, activation spreads outward along the paths of the network, but activation loses strength over distance.
     4. Model also assumes that activation decreases over time or intervening activity. This assumption places a constraint on the amount of activation that can occur, because activation of a second concept will decrease the amount of activation of the first concept.
     5. Success of any model depends on how well it can account for empirical results. One such result is the effect of *semantic priming*.
       a. Priming occurs when a decision about one concept makes it easier to decide about another concept.
       b. Mayer and Schvaneveldt's (1976) priming experiment
         i. Decide whether a string of letters made a word, e.g., *Butter* or *Nart*
         ii. Each trial consisted of a pair of strings, and the second string was presented immediately after people made their decision about the first string.
         iii. The most interesting results occurred when both strings were words.
         iv. If the two words were semantically related, people were much faster at verifying that the second string was a word than they were if the two words were unrelated.

6. The spreading activation model allows for the use of feature matching in verification of semantic statements.
   a. Therefore, it includes the assumptions of both Hierarchical Net models and Feature Comparison models.
   b. Collins and Loftus suggest that we consider the evidence obtained from both feature comparisons and superordinate links when we make a decision.
7. Criticism of Spreading Activation Model
   a. Too many assumptions — with enough assumptions can explain anything
   b. Too few clear-cut predictions — unless specific predictions can be tested, can't determine whether model's any good

III. Integration of Knowledge
A. ACT Model (Anderson, 1976)
1. Basic assumptions:
   a. Knowledge is stored in a semantic network consisting of interconnected nodes.
   b. Activation can spread down network paths from active nodes to activate new nodes and paths.
2. One application of this model is predicting how quickly people can retrieve stored information.
   a. Experiment:
      i. Learn 26 sentences of form "A [person] is in the [location]." For example, "A hippie is in the park," "A hippie is in the church," "A hippie is in the bank."
      ii. Particular individuals, e.g., "the hippie," and locations, e.g., the "bank," appeared either 1, 2, or 3 times among the 26 sentences.
      iii. After learning all 26 target sentences, the subjects were given a set of test sentences and asked to respond "true" to the target sentences and "false" to all other sentences in the test set.
   b. Anderson found that RT increased as the number of times a person or a location had appeared among the original sentences increased.
   c. Anderson interpreted results: time it takes to verify "the hippie is in park" depends on
      i. Rate at which activation spreads from two concepts
      ii. Length of path joining two concepts
      iii. Number of possible alternative paths activation can take

       d. ACT predicts RT should increase as number of links to either person or location increase.
          i. activation divides (fans out) among links.
          ii. called the *"fan effect"*

B. Modification of ACT -- Do more facts always increase retrieval time?
1. Related vs. unrelated facts were studied.
2. As the number of <u>unrelated</u> facts increased so did retrieval time.
3. Adding related facts did <u>not</u> increase retrieval time.
4. Anderson added the concept of *subnodes* to the ACT model. Subnodes are used to integrate related material.

C. Schema Theory
1. Schemas are organized structures that allow/help you to make sense out of new information.
2. Contrast between Bartlett's Schema Theory and the stimulus-response (S-R) approach

Schema Theory	S-R Approach
molar	atomistic
nonassociationistic	associationistic
generic	particular
active	passive

3. Modern Schema Theory
    a. Rumelhart (1980) argued that schema are the building blocks of cognition.
    b. Schema are used to interpret sensory data, retrieve information from LTM, organize actions, and solve problems.
    c. An advantage of having schematic knowledge is having *default knowledge*

4. *Scripts*: Representing sequences of events
    a. Shank and Abelson (1977) proposed the idea that knowledge is organized in terms of scripts.
       i. Roles, props/objects, conditions, results
       ii. Sequences of events
    b. Galambos and Rips (1982) tested whether scripts are organized temporally or around central actions.
       i. They asked students to rank-order script actions both for temporal order and centrality.
       ii. Other students asked to respond as quickly as possible whether an action/script pair belong together, e.g., Go to a restaurant/eat = "yes" vs. Go to a restaurant/fold clothes = "no."

  iii. If scripts are organized on basis of temporal order, they predict that it will be faster to verify pairs that contain actions which occur earlier in sequence than later actions.

  iv. If scripts are organized on basis of importance of each action to the goal of the script, they predict that it will be faster to verify pairs which contain important actions rather than those containing unimportant actions.

  v. Results: More important (central) actions verified more quickly. Temporal order unrelated to RTs.

 c. S.J. Anderson and M. A. Conway (1993)

  i. People identified the first autobiographical memory that came to mind for a specified time period.

  ii. Subjects either asked to recall in temporal order or by importance (centrality)

  iii. Results: More actions were listed when recall was temporal than when it was by centrality.

 d. Resolution of conflicting results: Faster access for more central actions. Once a script is found, faster search if temporally guided.

CHAPTER 9: PRACTICE QUESTIONS (Answers and page references are on p. 173.)

Multiple Choice Questions: For each question, circle the single, best alternative.

1. The more links that must be navigated to traverse a path between two concepts,

   a. the slower a subject's responses will be.
   b. the faster a subject's responses will be.
   c. the more likely a subject is to believe the concepts are related.
   d. the more closely associated the two concepts are.

2. The activation of one concept can lead to activation of other related concepts. This is called

   a. hierarchical activation.
   b. spreading activation.
   c. knowledge activation.
   d. schema activation.

3. Information is recalled better if it presented in a ___ fashion than if it is presented in a _____ fashion.

   a. random; hierarchical
   b. hierarchical; random
   c. hierarchical; semantic
   d. semantic; hierarchical

4. Students who are asked to recall categorical information (e.g., colors of the rainbow) generally pause between every

   a. item.
   b. 3 items.
   c. 5 items.
   d. 7 items.

5. Students who are taught to construct semantic networks recall more information than control students when they receive

   a. essay exams.
   b. multiple-choice exams.
   c. both *a* and *b*
   d. neither *a* nor *b*

6. Examples of hierarchical relations are

   a. "part" and "type."
   b. "part" and "characteristic."
   c. "type" and "leads to."
   d. "characteristic" and "leads to."

7. Organization of information in LTM is most often evaluated by asking students

   a. how they organize information.
   b. to verify semantic statements.
   c. to construct semantic networks.
   d. All of the above are used equally often.

8. According to the hierarchical network model, retrieval of the fact that a salmon swims requires

   a. no inferences.
   b. one inference.
   c. two inferences.
   d. four inferences.

9. Hierarchical networks store property information

   a. only at the highest level of the hierarchy.
   b. only at the lowest level of the hierarchy.
   c. redundantly; each property is represented at every level to which it is belongs.
   d. economically; each property is stored at the highest level for which it applies to all levels below.

10. According to the Hierarchical Network Model, it should take ___ to verify that a *Collie is a dog* than to verify that a *Collie can bark.*

    a. more time
    b. equal time
    c. less time
    d. can't tell which will take more time without knowing how the information in the individual's LTM is organized.

11. If a subject is faster at verifying that beer is a drink than that beer is a liquor, this is an example of the

    a. typicality effect.
    b. reversal of the typicality effect.
    c. category size effect.
    d. reversal of the category size effect.

12. According to the Feature Comparison Model, deciding that a collie is not a bird should be a fast decision because

    a. only defining features are considered.
    b. overall feature similarity is high.
    c. overall feature similarity is low.
    d. people "just know" that a collie isn't a bird.

13. According to the Feature Comparison Model, when a decision must be made about two concepts of intermediate similarity, only _____ are considered.

    a. defining features
    b. characteristic features
    c. both *a* and *b*
    d. neither *a* nor *b*

14. A difference between the Spreading Activation and Hierarchical Network models is that

    a. in the Hierarchical Network model concepts are represented as lists of features.
    b. in the Spreading Activation model concepts are represented as lists of features.
    c. in the Hierarchical Network model all links are the same length.
    d. in the Spreading Activation model all links are the same length.

15. Semantic priming occurs when

    a. making a decision about one concept makes it easier to make a decision about another concept.
    b. making a decision about one concept makes it harder to make a decision about another concept.
    c. entering the first stage of the feature comparison model.
    d. entering the second stage of the feature comparison model.

16. The slower spreading of activation when there are more links to a concept is called

    a. semantic priming.
    b. the typicality effect.
    c. the fan effect.
    d. the category size effect.

17. Increasing the number of pieces of information that a person has to learn

    a. always produces longer verification times.
    b. always produces shorter verification times.
    c. produces longer verification times if the pieces of information are related.
    d. none of the above

18. Which characteristic describes a schema?

    a. atomistic
    b. associationistic
    c. particularistic
    d. active

19. Suppose a friend tells you all about having dinner at the ABC restaurant but doesn't mention having ordered her meal. Your assumption that she must have ordered is based on

    a. spreading activation.
    b the fan effect.
    c. default knowledge.
    d. autobiographical memory.

20. Research on autobiographical memory has shown that the most important factor in determining how quickly people can access their memories is

    a. temporal order.
    b. centrality of events.
    c. whether the memories are positive.
    d. both *a* and *b*

True-False Questions:

T F   1.   The Spreading Activation Model is a kind of semantic network.

T F   2.   According to the Feature Comparison model, "can fly" is a characteristic feature of birds.

T F   3.   Parts and subparts of sentences are objective units that can simply be counted.

T F   4.   Verifying that a canary can fly requires making 1 inference.

T F   5.   Retrieving one concept from LTM should reduce the amount of time required to retrieve a related concept.

T F   6.   According to Anderson, schemata are the building blocks of cognition.

T F   7.   A criticism of the Hierarchical Network model is that it can't account for the category size effect.

T F   8.   The fan effect refers to faster verification times when related concepts are evaluated.

T F   9.   Subnodes were introduced into the ACT model to account for integration of information.

T F   10.   Scripts represent sequences of events that make up everyday activities.

Essay Questions:

1. Compare (identify both similarities and differences) the Hierarchical Network and Feature Comparison models.

2. Explain how schematic knowledge/scripts can facilitate everyday communication.

CHAPTER 10: LANGUAGE

I. **Three Aspects of Language:**
  A. **Grammar (Forming phrases)**
    1. Associationism (Skinner) believed that language was learned by learning associations between words in sentence.
    2. Chomsky found several problems with Behaviorist approach:
      a. Infinite number of sentences in all languages (how do you learn all associations?)
      b. Relations between nonadjacent words exist.
      c. Sentences have hierarchical structure.
  B. **Meaning (Combining words and morphemes)**
    1. Not all grammatically correct sentences <u>mean</u> something.
    2. Grammar = syntax, Meaning = semantics
    3. Biological evidence for distinction
      a. *Broca's aphasia* (halting, ungrammatical but meaningful speech)
      b. *Wernicke's aphasia* (grammatical, meaningless speech)
    4. Morphemes are the smallest units of language that carry meaning.
      a. Stem words
      b. Prefixes
      c. Suffixes
      d. Morphemes allow us to generate novel words, e.g., hydro+plane = hydroplane and aqua+lung = aqualung
  C. **Sound (Producing Phonemes)**
    1. At birth infants can discriminate among phonemes of all languages.
    2. By 6 months, infants have formed prototypes for phonemes of their native language. Causes perceptual magnet effect (inability to discriminate among sounds representing same phoneme)
  D. **Evidence for Heirarchical Organization (Speech Errors)**
    1. Slips of the tongue
    2. Exchange errors
      a. Word exchanges
      b. Morpheme exchanges
      c. Phoneme exchanges

II. **Psychology and Grammar**

A. Phrase Structure Grammar

1. Alternative to representing language as a string of words (the behaviorist/associationistic approach) is representing it as a rule system.
2. An example is shown in Figure 10.4, p. 253 of the text.
    a. The diagram, which is based on a set of rules, provides a picture of the grammatical organization.
    b. Rules are part of what is called *phrase structure grammar* because they reveal how we can form phrases consisting of groups of words.

B. Transformational Grammar

1. Problems with phrase structure grammar that led Chomsky to propose Transformational Grammar in 1957:
    a. No way to specify how a sentence can be modified to form a similar sentence:
        i.   Given "The boy hit the ball."
        ii. Active to passive, e.g., "The ball was hit by the boy."
        iii. Positive to negative, e.g., "The boy did not hit the ball."
        iv. Assertion to question, e.g., "Did the boy hit the ball?"
        v.   Consider the first transformation (active to passive).
            1. Transformation rule is: NP1 + V + NP2 ™ NP2 + was + V + by + NP1
            2. Transformation rule says invert position of two noun phrases and insert additional words (was, by) into sentence to make it passive.
    b. Not all sentences produced using phrase structure grammar make sense.
2. Another problem with both phrase structure grammar and Chomsky's early version of Transformational Grammar was that it could not always distinguish between different meanings of *ambiguous sentences.*
3. In 1965, Chomsky modified his transformational grammar to include notions of *deep structure* and *surface structure*.
    a. Deep structure represents <u>meaning</u> only -- it's <u>not</u> represented in words.
    b. Surface structure is related to sentence as it is heard.

        c. Resolving ambiguity may require knowledge of which deep structure is intended.

C. Ambiguous Sentences and Grammar
1. Types of ambiguity:
    a. Lexical - word has two meanings
    b. Surface - different meanings correspond to different sentence diagrams
    c. Underlying - different meanings have the same diagram, but the deep structure differs
2. Effects of ambiguity on comprehension: two alternative hypotheses
    a. People never notice ambiguities and simply activate one meaning, and therefore complete ambiguous sentences as quickly as they do closely related unambiguous ones.
    b. Ambiguity slows down processing.
3. McKay (1966) gave either ambiguous or unambiguous versions of same sentence stems and measured time-to-completion.
    a. No differences among unambiguous control sentences.
    b. All ambiguous sentences took longer to complete than nonambiguous.
    c. Lexical ambiguity is easiest to resolve; sentences with multiple ambiguities were most difficult.
    d. Although ambiguity slowed people down, only a few participants reported noticing it.

D. Words as Grammatical Clues
1. Words provide clues about grammatical structure (e.g., animate and inanimate nouns lead to different predictions about what will follow).
2. Readers' have implicit knowledge about how often different kinds of grammatical structures follow certain words.
3. Eye movements indicate that readers slow down when their predictions are violated.

III. Using Semantic Context in Sentence Comprehension

A. **Semantic Context and Word Recognition — (See for example, "went" vs. "event" in Figure 10.7, p. 2662)**
   1. Schwanenflugel and Shoben (1985) used a *lexical decision task.*
      a. *High constraint* vs. neutral context
      b. Expected vs. Unexpected target words
   2. Results:
      a. High constraint = better on expected and worse on unexpected than controls
      b. Low constraint = moderate facilitation for both expected and unexpected
   3. Explanation:
      a. activation of semantic features
      b. more activation for high constraint contexts

B. **Semantic Context and Ambiguous Meanings**
   1. Swinney and Hakes (1976)
      a. Two tasks:
         i.   Primary task was a sentence comprehension task.
         ii. Secondary task was a phoneme monitoring task.
      b. Performance on phoneme monitoring task is worse when the sentence contains an ambiguous word than when an unambiguous synonym is substituted.
      c. When the preceding context clarifies the meaning of the ambiguous word, there is no difference in performance of the phoneme monitoring task.
   2. Swinney (1979) used a *lexical decision task* to explore the effects of context on ambiguity resolution.
      a. Context: we were sitting on the bank
      b. Target words: appropriate = grass, inappropriate = money, neutral = glass)

    c. Results:

No delay between context and target word
appropriate word produces	priming
inappropriate word produces	priming
neutral word produces	no priming

4 syllable (750-1,000 msec) delay between context and target word
appropriate word produces	priming
inappropriate word produces	no priming
neutral word produces	no priming

C. Individual Differences in Resolving Ambiguities
    1. Good readers
        a. Fixate on and encode each word
        b. Encoding activates concepts (brings them into working memory).
        c. Integrate concept(s) with previous text
        d. If compatible then used further, if incompatible then a decay in activation will occur (suppression of inappropriate meanings).
        e. Have a *large working memory capacity* (can keep both or all meanings active until ambiguity resolved)
    2. Poor readers
        a. Are less able to suppress inappropriate meanings which means they have to activate error recovery procedures (see Figure 10.6, p. 259 of text)
        b. Have a small working memory (only one meaning retained -- usually the dominant one)
D. Syntactic Processing
    1. Syntactic ambiguity occurs when we are uncertain about the grammatical structure of a sentence.
    2. Degree of activation of alternate structures is affected by both prior context and the frequency of alternate structures.

IV. Implications of Sentences

A. People often fail to distinguish between implied and direct statements.

1. Bransford, Barclay, and Franks (1972) presented subjects with lists of sentences to memorize.
   a. After the subjects indicated that they had memorized the sentences, they were asked to say which sentences they had seen before (say "New") and which they had not (say "Old").
   b. Results: subjects nearly always "recognized" sentences which were implied by the sentences experienced in the experiment even though they actually had not been presented.

B. Courtroom Testimony

   a. Loftus' (1975) work has shown that "leading" questions influence eyewitness testimony.
   b. Harris (1978) found that 64% of implied statements were rated as "true" by jurors even though they were never asserted.

C. Advertising Claims -- even when forewarned and allowed to make immediate judgments, 50% of implied advertising claims were accepted as true (Harris, 1977).

CHAPTER 10: PRACTICE QUESTIONS (Answers and page references are on p. 174.)

Multiple Choice Questions: For each question, circle the single, best alternative.

1. The smallest units of language that carry meaning are called

    a. morphemes.
    b. phonemes.
    c. phonetic elements.
    d. words.

2. Syntax is

    a. the rules governing the sequence of words in forming phrases and sentences.
    b. the rules governing the change from one sentence form to another, e.g., passive to active.
    c. the rules governing the disambiguation of ambiguous sentences.
    d. all of the above

3. Sentences like "Colorless green ideas sleep furiously" indicate that

    a. not all sentences need to have a verb phrase.
    b. it is possible for a sentence to have an irregular phrase structure.
    c. the semantic content of a sentence governs its syntactic form.
    d. a sentence can be grammatical even if it is meaningless.

4. Aphasia is the

   a. disruption of language skills caused by damage to the brain.
   b. loss of memory caused by damage to the brain.
   c. disruption of motor skills caused by damage to the brain.
   d. all of the above

5. What is the "strange and miraculous gift" to which Steven referred?

   a. grammar
   b. language
   c. meaning
   d. sound

6. Which of the following changes does not require a transformation rule?

   a. rewriting a sentence as a noun phrase and a verb phrase
   b. rewriting an active sentence as a passive sentence
   c. rewriting a negative sentence as a question
   d. rewriting a question as an active sentence

7. Eye movement analysis indicates that readers slow down more when reading "The defendant examined by the lawyer…" than when they read "The evidence examined by the lawyer…" What does this tell us about language processing?

   a. aphasics have trouble processing animate nouns
   b. there is a perceptual magnet effect
   c. speech is hierarchically organized
   d. words create syntactic expectations

8. What kinds of errors indicate that language is hierarchically arranged?

   a. ambiguity errors
   b. aphasic errors
   c. exchange errors
   d. syntactic errors

9. Which of the following is an example of a high-constraint sentence?

   a. Mary put her stuff in the _____.
   b. I took cooking classes in _____.
   c. John left his keys at the _____.
   d. Ellen put the picture in a _____.

10. Comprehension of syntactic ambiguity can be affected by

    a. context.
    b. frequency.
    c. both *a* and *b*
    d. neither *a* nor *b*

11. Language is

    a. symbolic.
    b. generative.
    c. structured.
    d. all of the above

12. As individuals mature they become

    a. better able to distinguish the phonemes that make up all the languages of the world.
    b. better able to distinguish variants of the phonemes that make up their native language.
    c. less able to distinguish variants of the phonemes that make up their native language.
    d. both *a* and *b*

13. Which of the following is an unlikely slip of the tongue?

    a. "skort shirt" for "short skirt"
    b. "a tea of cup" for "a cup of tea"
    c. "breaks the bounding" for "breaking the bounds"
    d. "chalk and tout" for "talk and touch"

14. According to Chomsky, the expression of meaningful ideas is a result of what?

    a. combining syntax and semantics appropriately
    b. combining lexicon and semantics appropriately
    c. combining syntax and lexicon appropriately
    d. all of the above

15. Sentence comprehension consists of

    a. fixation and encoding.
    b. retrieving meaning.
    c. integrating meaning and prior context.
    d. all of the above

16. Context can inhibit comprehension when ___ word is encountered in a _____ context

    a. an expected; low-constraint
    b. an unexpected; low-constraint
    c. an expected; high-constraint
    d. an unexpected; high-constraint

17. When an ambiguous word is preceded by a context that makes its meaning clear, performance on a phoneme-monitoring task is _____ relative to a control condition.

    a. negatively affected
    b. not affected
    c. positively affected
    d. none of the above

18. Asking subjects to make immediate judgments about whether implied statements are true produces

    a. no errors.
    b. very few errors.
    c. less than 50% errors.
    d. more than 50% errors.

19. Which of the following is <u>not</u> a morpheme?

    a. ing
    b   ph
    c. pre
    d. word

20. Which of the following is <u>not</u> a kind of exchange error?

    a. morpheme exchange
    b. phoneme exchange
    c. syntax exchange
    d. word exchange

True-False Questions:

T F   1.   People can easily distinguish between asserted and implied statements.

T F   2.   Grammatical sentences are meaningful.

T F   3.   Wernicke's aphasia occurs when speech is grammatical but doesn't convey much semantic content.

T F   4.   Phrase structure grammar represents language as a rule system.

T F   5.   Comprehension is only influenced by prior context.

T F   6.   Poor readers often have to engage in error recovery heuristics because they can't maintain the multiple meanings of an ambiguous word in working memory.

T F   7.   Immediately after an ambiguous word was presented in a sentence that made clear which meaning was intended, subjects making lexical decisions responded faster to contextually appropriate words than to contextually inappropriate words.

T F   8.   When syntactic expectations are violated, people read sentences just as quickly as when their expectations are not violated.

T F   9.   False recognitions are a problem when the presented sentences do not imply the test sentences.

T F   10.   Changing the article used in a question (e.g., "the" for "a") can change the response obtained from an eyewitness.

Essay Questions:

1. Summarize the research describing the effects of semantic context on comprehension.

2. What evidence indicates that people have a very difficult time separating implications from direct statements?

CHAPTER 11: COMPREHENSION AND MEMORY FOR TEXT

I. **Prior Knowledge of the Reader:**
   A. **Effect of Prior Knowledge on Comprehension**
      1. Bransford and Johnson (1973) presented subjects with a short story (quoted material on pp. 275-276) with 14 *idea units*.
         a. Three conditions:
            i. Context before reading
            ii. Context after reading
            iii. No context
         b. Results:

Condition	mean ideas recalled
Context before reading	8.0
Context after reading	3.6
No context at all	3.6

      2. Bransford and Johnson (1973) also presented subjects with a short description (one long paragraph) of doing the laundry (quoted material on p. 277).
         a. Three conditions:
            i. Title before reading
            ii. Title after reading
            iii. No Title
         b. Results:

Condition	mean ideas recalled
Title before reading	5.8
Title after reading	2.7
No title at all	2.8

   B. **Effect of Prior Knowledge on Retrieval -- Anderson and Pichert (1978) demonstrated that even when material is easily comprehended initially, context affects recall.**
      1. The story contained 72 ideas.
      2. The 72 ideas had been rated by a group of students who had rated them for their importance to a burglar (e.g., no one home on Thurs.) or to a homeowner (e.g., leaky roof).
      3. Context at learning was manipulated (pretend to be a burglar vs. a homeowner).
      4. Recall tested
      5. Context either reinstated or changed
      6. Recall was tested again.

   a. Change in context results in a 7-10% increase in ideas recalled
   b. Same context actually produces slightly worse recall
  7. Possible Explanations:
   a. Guessing
   b. Change in criterion for reporting
   c. New plan for searching memory
  8. Based on subject reports, the latter (7c) is most likely.

C. Effect of Prior Knowledge on False Recognition and Recall
  1. Sulin and Dooling (1974) presented same short story about a dictator to two groups of subjects.
   a. Group 1 told story about "Gerald Martin" (fictitious).
   b. Group 2 told story was about Adolph Hitler.
   c. Students were tested for recognition memory after either a five-minute or one-week delay.
    i. Testing involved 7 sentences from original story and 7 sentences not in original story.
    ii. Of those sentences that were not included in the original story, 4 were neutral, and 1 each was of high (e.g., hated Jews), medium (e.g., wanted to conquer world), or low (e.g., intelligent, not kind) relatedness to Hitler.
   d. After the 5 min. delay, there was no effect of title on recognition (few false positives).
   e. After the one-week delay, both medium- and highly-related false sentences were incorrectly recognized. Many more for the Hitler-labeled than for the Gerald Martin-labeled version.
  2. Script knowledge also can lead to false recall and recognition.
   a. Subjects were asked to list events related to either a robbery or a mugging.
   b. Four of those events were directly stated by an eyewitness and four were not.
   c. One week later, the participants were asked to recall the eyewitness's statements.
    i. 31% of the direct statements were correctly recalled.
    ii. 15% of the unstated events were falsely recalled.
    iii. When an attorney attempted to mislead the participants, 25% of the unstated events were falsely recalled.

3. In summary, prior knowledge influences comprehension in a variety of ways.
   a. Makes the abstract easier to understand
   b. Determines what is emphasized and provides a framework for recall
   c. May inhibit performance if performance requires distinguishing between old and new knowledge

II. **Organization of the Text**
   A. **In order to understand a story, one must organize information at two levels: (1) Global and (2) Local.**
      1. *Global Coherence* refers to making sense of (connecting to one another) the main events that occur throughout the story.
      2. *Local Coherence* refers to making sense of (connecting to one another) the most recent events in the story.
      3. Both are affected by organization of the text.
   B. **Story Structure**
      1. *Setting* -- time, location, major characters
      2. *Theme* -- general focus, often the goal of main character
      3. *Plot* -- series of actions main character takes to achieve goal
      4. *Resolution* -- did main character succeed?
      5. Placing goal information at the end of a story reduces recall and failing to mention goal reduces recall even further. (Thorndyke, 1977)
      6. Bower, Black and Turner have tested the hypothesis that goals are particularly important by studying memory for "script"-type story information.
         a. Information consisted of:
            i. Interruptions (*obstacles*)
            ii. Script relevant facts (expected)
            iii. Irrelevant facts
         b. Results:
            i. Interruptions (obstacles):   53% recall
            ii. Script relevant (expected):   38% recall
            iii. Irrelevant: 32% recall
   C. **Causal Connections**
      1. Judged importance increases with the number of causal connections related to statement.
      2. Number of causal connections also predicts how quickly information can be recalled (more = faster).

D. Integration of Details/Local Coherence
1. Three factors affect comprehension difficulty:
   a. Are ideas "old" or "new"?
   b. Integration is easier if information is carried from one sentence to the next.
      i. Are related ideas in STM? If not, then integration is difficult. (Requires a *reinstatement search*)
      ii. Can ideas be directly linked? If not, then integration requires inferences and is more difficult.
   c. Lesgold, Roth, and Curtis (1979) manipulated ease of integration of two sentences (see examples on p. 338 of text). Results: Comprehension of final sentence was faster for example #3 than for example #2. Example #1 produces fastest RTs.

III. Kintsch's Model of Comprehension
A. Processing Assumptions
1. Two inputs to model: Reader and Text
   a. Reader brings goals and knowledge that affect "relevance", expectations, and inferences.
   b. Text consists of *propositions* (meaningful units of words).
      i. Model specifies rules for dividing text into propositions.
      ii. Propositions are interconnected in a network (like a semantic network).
2. Important parameter in model is *number of propositions that are active in STM* (working memory) -- limited capacity STM.
3. As one reads:
   a. Encode first sentence as a set of propositions
   b. Select most important propositions to retain in STM (goals, prior knowledge, title, etc. affect choice)
   c. Encode next sentence as a set of propositions
   d. Try to connect new propositions to propositions already in STM
      i. If a word (or words) matches then connection can be made (understanding has occurred).
      ii. If no two concepts match, then see if new propositions are related to contents of LTM. This is called a *reinstatement search*.
         1. If found in LTM, bring into working memory (reinstate) and connect new propositions to old.
         2. If no match is found in LTM, must make an inference about how the two are related.

4. Major thrust of model is that understanding occurs more easily if the coherence graph (representation of the connections among propositions) is easily built.
5. If inferences or reinstatement searches are necessary, comprehension will be more difficult.

B. Predicting Readability
1. Dependent variable is the number of propositions recalled divided by reading time.
2. Two best predictors are:
   a. Word frequency (familiarity)
   b. Number of reinstatement searches required
3. Number of inferences required also predicts readability (but not as well).

C. Incorporating Prior knowledge
1. *Situation model* in which prior knowledge is combined with text information
2. Increasing readability by reducing need for inferences
   a. Britton and Gulgoz (1991) modified a text passage describing the air war in North Vietnam.
      i. Found 40 instances where an inference was required and modified text so that no inferences were required.
      ii. People who read <u>original</u> text recalled 3.44 propositions/minute reading time.
      iii. People who read <u>modified</u> text recalled 5.24 propositions/minute reading time.
   b. Kintsch (1994) modified a text passage describing the functioning of a faulty heart.
      i. As Britton and Gulgoz found, modified text produced greater recall.
      ii. However, <u>performance on problem solving questions interacted with knowledge of reader</u>. Low-knowledge readers did better with modified text.
      High-knowledge readers did better with original text.

CHAPTER 11: PRACTICE QUESTIONS (Answers and page references are on p. 175.)

Multiple Choice Questions: For each question, circle the single, best alternative.

1. Comprehension is most difficult when information in the story is

   a. directly related to previous information stored in STM.
   b. directly related to information stored in LTM.
   c. indirectly related to previous information in STM.
   d. indirectly related to previous information in LTM.

2. Providing a context after a subject has read an abstract, unfamiliar passage

   a. produces recall that is comparable to a context-before condition.
   b. produces recall that is comparable to a no-context condition.
   c. improves recall but not as much as when the context is provided before reading.
   d. none of the above

3. Providing a context before reading abstract text is necessary for good comprehension of

   a. unfamiliar content.
   b. familiar content.
   c. both *a* and *b*
   d. neither *a* nor *b*

4. New information is integrated into existing information such that they are indistinguishable

   a. immediately.
   b. within five minutes.
   c. within one week.
   d. Never.

5. Changing perspective

   a. can aid in retrieving otherwise inaccessible information.
   b. does not affect retrieval of inaccessible information.
   c. only helps if the perspective was considered at the time of storage.
   d. only helps if the material is abstract and unfamiliar.

6. Script knowledge can

    a. improve eyewitness testimony.
    b. cause false recognition by an eyewitness.
    c. cause an eyewitness to falsely recall an event.
    d. both *b* and *c*

7. Global coherence refers to

    a. integrating recent events in a story.
    b. integrating the main events in a story.
    c. integrating the events in a paragraph.
    d. all of the above

8. One determinant of the way events in a text are organized is

    a. global coherence.
    b. local coherence.
    c. prior knowledge of the reader.
    d. story structure.

9. Placing the goal at the end of a simple narrative

    a. does not affect comprehension.
    b. enhances comprehension.
    c. reduces comprehension.
    d. is an example of standard story structure.

10. When asked to read script-based stories, the type of information people remember best is

    a. goal disruptions.
    b. irrelevant information.
    c. script actions.
    d. All of the above are remembered equally well.

11. A causal relation exists such that *A* causes *B* if

    a. *A* cannot occur without *B* also occurring.
    b. *B* cannot occur without *A* also occurring.
    c. *A* can occur without *B* but *B* cannot occur without *A*.
    d. *A* is sufficient but not necessary for the occurrence of *B*

12. The number of causal connections linked to a statement is a significant determinant of the statement's

    a. retrieval speed.
    b. importance.
    c. likelihood of being recalled.
    d. all of the above

13. Myers and his colleagues found that students were faster at deciding whether test sentences were true or false when they had studied

    a. three, low-integrated sentences.
    b. three, high-integrated sentences.
    c. six, low-integrated sentences.
    d. six, high-integrated sentences.

14. Local coherence is difficult to establish when the ideas in a current sentence

    a. are not related to the story's goal.
    b. are related to those in STM.
    c. were given in a previous sentence.
    d. are not related to those in the previous sentence.

15. Lesgold, Roth and Curtis (1979) found that inserting information between the two sentences, "A thick cloud of smoke hung over the forest," and "The forest was on fire,"

    a. did not affect comprehension of sentence two.
    b. always reduced comprehension of sentence two.
    c. reduced comprehension of sentence two if the insertions were irrelevant.
    d. reduced comprehension of sentence two if the insertions were relevant.

16. Making inferences in order to connect a current sentence to a previous one

    a. does not affect reading time.
    b. decreases reading time.
    c. increases reading time.
    d. could result in any of the above.

17. Propositions divide the text into meaningful units. This is an important assumption of

    a. Anderson's model of the fan effect.
    b. Bransford and Johnson's model of text comprehension.
    c. Kintsch's model of text comprehension.
    d. Thorndyke's model of story structure.

18. Most readability formulas lack

    a. sentence variables.
    b. text organization variables.
    c. word variables.
    d. none of the above

19. The number of propositions recalled multiplied by reading time is a measure of

    a. comprehension.
    b intelligence.
    c. readability.
    d. none of the above

20. Reducing the number of inferences required to comprehend a text is

    a. always beneficial.
    b. always harmful.
    c. sometimes harmful for low-knowledge readers.
    d. sometimes harmful for high-knowledge readers.

True-False Questions:

T F   1. Reading speed can be used as a measure of comprehension.

T F   2. Contexts for abstract material are equally useful when provided either before and after the material is read.

T F   3. The kind of information that one recalls can reflect the perspective that one adopts.

T F   4. Subjects who read a story about Gerald Martin falsely recognized high-related decoy sentences one week later.

T F   5. The introduction of misleading information by an attorney doesn't affect false recognitions.

T F   6. The optimal order of story components is setting, plot, theme, and resolution.

T F   7. The judged importance of actions is directly related to the number of causal connections associated with that action.

T F   8. If the information in a current sentence is new, it will be easy to integrate into the previous sentences.

T F   9. Mental models keep track of information about the main characters in stories.

T F   10. Kintsch's model of text comprehension assumes that reader and text variables interact to determine readability.

Essay Questions:

1. A friend of yours wants to write a third-grade textbook. Based on what you learned from this chapter, what can you tell your friend about increasing the readability of the text?

.

2. Summarize Kintsch's model of text comprehension.

CHAPTER 12: PROBLEM SOLVING

I. **Classifying Problems:**
   A. **Greeno (1978) defined problems in terms of cognitive abilities required to solve problems.**
   B. **He argues that there are three classes of specific problem-related cognitive abilities.**
   C. ***Arrangement Problems***
      1. Task: to find a new arrangement/relation among the components
      2. Provided: To-be-rearranged components and criteria for the solution
      3. Skills required:
         a. Fluency in generating possibilities
         b. Retrieval of solution patterns (analogy, etc.)
         c. Knowledge of principles constraining the search
      4. Gestalt psychologists emphasized problem structure and, therefore, analyzed problem solving from this perspective.
         a. Correct organization often results from *insight*
         b. Insight causes a sudden solution due to reorganization of problem representation.
         c. *Functional fixedness* makes finding the correct arrangement difficult, e.g., Candle and String problems.
   D. ***Inducing Structure Problems***
      1. Task: to identify the principle/rule/underlying structure that explains how components are related
      2. Provided: Components organized according to principle/rule
      3. Skills required:
         a. Identifying relations among components
         b. Fitting relations into patterns
      4. Sternberg's model of analogical problem solving has four processes:
         a. Encoding (What's important?)
         b. Inference (What is/are the relevant relation(s) between 1st and 2nd terms?)
         c. Mapping (What is/are the relevant relation(s) between 1st and 3rd terms?)
         d. Application (What is the relevant relation between 3rd and 4th terms?)

132

E. *Transformation Problems*
  1. Task: To transform initial state into a specified goal state
  2. Provided: explicit description of start state, explicit description of goal state, permissible/legal operators
  3. Skills required: planning based on *means-end analysis*
  4. Most studied class of problems. It's highly amenable to computer programming. Most problem-solving theories are based on this kind of problem.

II. **Newell and Simon's Theory**
  A. **Objective and Method**
     1. Consider how programming a computer to solve problems could contribute to a theory of human problem solving (*simulation programming*).
     2. Collect detailed data on how humans solve the same problems (*verbal protocols*).
     3. Why computers?
        a. In general, thinking is not directly observable.
        b. Simulation programs precisely define terms like "memory" and "strategy."
        c. If the computer program works, this means that no steps have been left unspecified.
        d. Success of the computer program in solving the problem is a *measure of sufficiency.*
  B. **Theoretical Assumptions**
     1. Performance is limited by capacity, storage time, and retrieval time of both STM and LTM.
     2. A good plan for solving a problem ignores unpromising choices.
        a. Problem itself determines the number of possible paths and choices that exist.
        b. Problem solver determines which of these should be explored (*problem space*).
        c. Factors that affect the problem solver's choices are:
           i. Instructions
           ii. Previous experience with identical or nearly identical task
           iii. Previous experience with analogous tasks
           iv. General strategies stored in LTM
           v. Information acquired while solving problem

C. *Means-end Analysis*
1. Most studied problem-solving technique
   a. Amenable to being programmed
   b. Frequently used by novices
2. Find, identify, and reduce differences.
   a. Explicitly guided by goal
   b. Initial goal may lead to subgoals (decomposition).
   c. Method can be applied recursively (over and over again).
   d. May lead to dead ends.
3. *Operators* are permissible changes in the problem state.
4. *Table of Connections* shows the relation between operators and differences in problem states.

III. General Strategies
A. *Algorithms*
1. Guarantee solution if applied correctly. E.g., multiplication rules, factoring rules
2. May be time-consuming
3. Must be used systematically
B. *Heuristics* are basic guidelines/rules. E.g., check the plug, try the easier solution first, etc.
1. *Subgoals* (problem state(s) that one must pass through to attain goal)
   a. may not be easy to identify.
   b. reduce amount of problem space because subgoals reduce number of sequential choices.
   c. One must apply other heuristics to attain each of the subgoals.
2. *Analogy* (Recognize similarity and apply known solution)
   a. Heavy reliance on LTM
   b. Not commonly used, e.g., Gick and Holyoak (1980)
3. *Diagrams*
   a. External memory function
   b. Shows relation(s) among problem components
   c. Thomas, Carroll, and Malhotra's (1980) research on spatial and temporal analogs showed that use of diagrams improved problem solving performance.
C. *Representational Transfer* is the transfer of general problem solving methods (Novick, 1990).
1. Diagrammatic representations help to represent the underlying structure of problems.
   a. Network
   b. Hierarchy
   c. Venn Diagram

2. Three conditions:
   a. Control
   b. Relevant example with <u>no hint</u> that it might useful for solving the current problem
   c. Relevant example with <u>hint</u> that it might be useful for solving the current problem
3. Results:
   a. No difference between control subjects and those not informed of usefulness of the example.
   b. Success of the hint depended on the kind of relevant representation.
4. Novick and Hurley (2001) identified 10 characteristics that might distinguish matrix, network and hierarchical representations, e.g., the number and type of connections among nodes.
   a. Asked students to choose what kind of representation they would use to organize the information in 18 short scenarios
   b. Students mentioned nine of the ten properties among when justifying their choices.

CHAPTER 12: PRACTICE QUESTIONS (Answers and page references are on p. 176.)

Multiple Choice Questions: For each question, circle the single, best alternative.

1. A problem solving heuristic

    a. is guaranteed to find a problem solution, if one exists.
    b. is a strategy that guides a search through the problem space.
    c. is likely to be less effective than a strategy such as means-end analysis.
    d. is needed for unfamiliar problems, but not for familiar problems.

2. Verbal protocols are

    a. detailed records of what subjects say when asked to think aloud while working on a problem.
    b. the output from computer models programmed to simulate human problem solving.
    c. procedures designed by problem solving experts.
    d. reports by the subject, after the problem has been solved, about which strategies worked and which didn't.

3. The tendency to be rigid in how one thinks about an object's uses is called

    a. functional fixedness.
    b. functional narrowness.
    c. mental stickiness.
    d. narrow focus.

4. Which of the following is an algorithm?

    a. analogy
    b. diagrams
    c. multiplication
    d. subgoals

5. Anne's baby needed diapering but she didn't have a diaper. Anne used a kitchen towel in place of a diaper. In this instance, Anne

    a. is applying a problem-solving algorithm.
    b. has solved the problem by using functional fixedness.
    c. has managed to overcome functional fixedness.
    d. is making the best possible use of her kitchen towel.

6. Who claimed that problem
solving can be viewed as the
"most characteristically human
activity"?

   a. Greeno
   b. Newell
   c. Polya
   d. Sternberg

7. Puzzles are used to study
problem solving

   a. to identify individual
differences.
   b. to eliminate individual
differences.
   c. to study expertise.
   d. both *a* and *c*

8. Which of the following is an
example of an arrangement
problem?

   a. anagram
   b. analogy
   c. missionaries and cannibals
   d. Raven's progressive matrices

9. Which of the following is not a
skill that is used to solve
arrangement problems?

   a. fluency in generating
possible solutions
   b. identifying relation among
problem components
   c. knowledge of principles
limiting the search for
possible solutions
   d. retrieval of solution patterns

10. Insight is the

   a. "aha" moment in problem
solving.
   b. reorganized problem
structure.
   c. gradual accretion of a
problem solution.
   d. main component of means-
end analysis.

11. People are better able to solve
Duncker's candle problem when

   a. the boxes are empty.
   b. the boxes contained the other
solution components.
   c. they are given a hint to use
the screwdriver as a
pendulum.
   d. none of the above

12. Which of the following is an example of an inducing structure problem?

   a. candle problem
   b. jealous husbands
   c. series extrapolation
   d. water jars

13. Transformation problems differ from both arrangement and inducing structure problems because they

   a. require the ability to fit relations together.
   b. require retrieval of solution patterns.
   c. provide the goal.
   d. specify the initial problem state.

14. Newell and Simon argued that if a computer simulation correctly solved a problem, it was

   a. proof that this was how humans solved the problem.
   b. an indication that this might be how humans solved the same problem.
   c. to be considered intelligent.
   d. both *b* and *c*

15. The DONALD + GERALD = ROBERT problem was used by Newell and Simon to demonstrate that

   a. algorithms can limit the number of paths that must be searched.
   b. heuristics can limit the number of paths that must be searched.
   c. the number of incorrect paths determine problem difficulty.
   d. diagrams can be used to solve the problem.

16. Means-end analysis relies on

   a. operators.
   b. reducing the difference between the goal and the current state.
   c. table of connections.
   d. all of the above

17. A table-of-connections shows which _____can be eliminated by each of the_____.

   a. differences; general procedures
   b. differences; operators
   c. similarities; general procedures
   d. similarities; operators

18. Which of the following is an example of solving via analogy? Approaching unfamiliar problems by

    a. creating a graphical representation.
    b. checking LTM for knowledge of similar problems.
    c. dividing the problems into parts and trying to solve each part separately.
    d. starting at the goal and working back toward the current state.

19. Forming subgoals while problem solving

    a. guarantees an easier solution.
    b. means using diagrams.
    c. is often helpful.
    d. all of the above

20. Carroll, Thomas and Malhotra (1980) found that subjects who were not instructed to use a diagram to solve a temporal version of a problem

    a. satisfied more problem constraints than subjects given a spatial isomorph.
    b. satisfied fewer problem constraints than subjects given a spatial isomorph.
    c. solved more slowly than subjects given a spatial isomorph.
    d. both b and c

21. In a hierarchical model, how many paths are there from one node to another?

    c. None
    d. One
    e. Two
    f. More than two

True-False Questions:

T F 1. Greeno classified problems according to the cognitive skills required to solve them.

T F 2. According to Sternberg, the first step in solving an analogy problem is to identify the relation between the first two terms in the problem.

T F 3. Means-end analysis is STM-intensive.

T F 4. Newell and Simon used verbal protocols to evaluate computer simulations.

T F 5. Newell and Simon showed that algorithms can be used to reduce the search for a problem solution.

T F 6. The General Problem Solver was used to study a symbol manipulation task.

T F 7. The problem space that is explored is the same as the space determined by the problem.

T F 8. Subgoals reduced the use of a balance strategy by people trying to solve the missionaries and cannibals problem.

T F 9. The attack-dispersion problem and the radiation problem are analogous.

T F 10. Representational transfer involves remembering a specific solution and applying it to another problem.

Essay Questions:

1. Summarize the Newell and Simon model of problem solving.

2. Define representational transfer and analogical transfer. How do the two differ and how are they similar?

CHAPTER 13: EXPERTISE AND CREATIVITY

I. **Expertise and Reasoning**
   A. **Logical Reasoning**
      1. Wason's four-card selection task
         a. Each of four cards has a letter on one side and a number on the other (showing are D, K, 3, and 7).
         b. Subjects were asked which cards must be turned over to evaluate truth of a rule stating, "Every card that has a D on one side has a 3 on the other."
         c. Implications of <u>conditional</u> rule (If D then 3) are not clear to most people (only about 4% can solve).
      2. Wason and Johnson-Laird argued that errors are due to *confirmation-seeking*
         a. Seeking to verify rather than disconfirm
         b. Sensible in real world
      3. Wason and Shapiro hypothesized that errors are due to the abstract nature of task. They thought more realistic versions of problem would be simpler to solve. For example, "Every time I go to Manchester, I go by train." Results: 62.5% accurate with realistic, 12.5% with abstract
      4. Johnson-Laird and colleagues used the letter sorting task. This task was an accurate description of the British postal rules at the time. Results: 71% solutions for realistic version, 0% for abstract version of same problem
      5. Griggs and Cox suggested that one uses memory and not reasoning to solve familiar versions of the problems (*memory retrieval explanation*).
         a. Undergraduates at the University of Florida did just as badly on the letter sorting version of the problem (which was unfamiliar) as they did on the abstract version.
         b. However, the drinking-age version of the problem <u>is</u> familiar to them. Results: 72.5% solved drinking-age version, 0% solved abstract version
      6. Recently, Nisbett and his colleagues at the University of Michigan have proposed that we do have some abstract reasoning abilities (we don't always have to rely on memory or guess). *Pragmatic reasoning schemata*: general reasoning-structures that can be applied to many problems.

    a. *Permission schema:* fulfilling some prerequisite to obtain a goal, e.g., In order to obtain driver's license, one must pass the driver's test

    b. *Obligation schema:* an action is required if a prerequisite is fulfilled, e.g., If one's income is greater than $50,000, one must pay taxes

B. Analogical Reasoning
1. People rarely notice analogies spontaneously.
    a. Perhaps because different concepts are involved in the two problems
    b. Perhaps because they do not realize that they need help to solve a problem
2. Silver asked 7th graders to classify math problems that shared either solution procedures or problem contents, e.g.,

Solution Procedure	Problem Content			
	Animals	**Classes**	**Plants**	**People**
Addition	Prob. 1	Prob. 2	Prob. 3	Prob. 4
Subtraction	Prob. 6	Prob. 7	Prob. 8	Prob. 9
Multiplication	Prob. 10	Prob. 11	Prob. 12	Prob. 13
Division	Prob. 14	Prob. 15	Prob. 16	Prob. 17

    a. Results: Better problem solvers (experts) sort by solution procedure; poor solvers (novices) sort by content.
    b. Using recall as the dependent variable produces similar results. Novices recall more content; experts recall more about mathematical structure.
3. Similar results were found for physics and medicine

C. Scientific Reasoning
1. Two types of expertise are required for expert scientific reasoning:
    a. Knowledge of good experimental design
    b. Knowledge of specific hypothesis being tested
2. Schunn and Anderson compared the abilities of three groups of individuals:
    a. Cognitive psychology faculty who were memory experts (domain experts)
    b. Social and Developmental faculty who were not memory experts (task experts)
    c. A mixed group of undergraduates (high- and mid-ability)

3. Everyone was asked to design an experiment to test two alternative explanations of the spacing effect using a computer interface that allowed manipulation of three variables:
    a. number of repetitions
    b. spacing of repetitions
    c. change of context between repetitions
4. Both faculty and students were evaluated for domain-general skills that are required to design experiments and domain-specific skills that are useful in designing memory experiments.
    a. Memory experts had better domain-specific skills than any other group (all other groups were equal to one another).
    b. Faculty had better domain-general skills than either the high- or mid-ability students.

II. **Acquiring Expertise**
   A. **Search versus Implementation**: Gick's model of problem solving (Figure 13.3, p. 338)
      1. Construct a problem representation by identifying a connection to a known problem (this may activate existing schema).
      2. Search for a solution (requires the use of general strategies, e.g., means-end analysis).
      3. Implement solution.
      4. If a schema is activated as a result of constructing a problem representation, it may be possible to skip stage 2 and go directly to implementation.
   B. **Learning a Solution**
      1. Novices use general strategies, e.g., means-end analysis.
      2. Experts *work forward.*
      3. Students switch from means-end analysis to working forward as they become more experienced.
      4. Sweller has argued that although means-end analysis is an efficient way of obtaining a goal it is <u>not</u> an efficient way to learn the order of solution steps.
         a. Means-end analysis focuses on reducing differences.
         b. Means-end analysis is very memory intensive.
         c. 9 of 10 students assigned to a nongoal condition solved test problems by working forward while only 1 of 10 students assigned to a goal condition did so.

C. Combining Theory and Instruction: Anderson's ACT* model
1. ACT* consists of assumptions about declarative and procedural knowledge.
   a. *Declarative knowledge* is the representation and organization of factual knowledge, e.g., stop signs are red octagons.
   b. *Procedural knowledge* is the knowledge of how to use declarative knowledge to perform tasks.
2. Procedural component of the model consists of *production rules*.
   a. Rules take IF . . . THEN . . . form.
   b. The IF . . . part of a production rule specifies a goal.
   c. The THEN . . . part of a production rule specifies an action that will satisfy the goal.
   d. Mastery of hundreds of production rules is required to learn a complex skill.
   e. Production rules are organized according to a hierarchical goal structure.
3. According to the model, all knowledge begins as declarative knowledge. Declarative knowledge has to be converted into efficient procedures for solving specific problems.
4. The LISP (a programming language) Tutor consists of 1200 production rules that apply to programming in the LISP language.
   a. The tutor covers basic LISP concepts in a one-semester, self-paced course at Carnegie-Mellon.
   b. On average, students who use the tutor earn grades that are one letter grade higher than students who don't use the tutor.

III. **Creativity:** Creative solutions are both novel and useful.
   A. Constraining Effects of Examples: Smith, Ward, and Schumacher asked subjects to draw creatures that might live on another planet.
   1. They showed subjects 3 example creatures.
   2. People who saw the examples tended to draw similar creatures.
      a. If instructed not to copy and they were asked to produce their creatures immediately, they didn't copy the examples.
      b. If instructed not to copy but they weren't asked to produce their creatures until one day later, they did copy the examples (*inadvertent plagiarism?*).
   B. Inventing Objects through Imagery
   1. Subjects were shown basic parts, e.g., wire, tube, sphere, and cube.
   2. Told about 8 categories of objects, e.g., furniture, and assigned to one of three conditions.
      a. Subject chose 3 of the basic parts and was assigned a category of object to produce.

      b. Subject was assigned to use 3 of the basic parts and chose a category of object to produce.

      c. Subject was assigned both parts and category (most restrictive condition).

  3. Asked to close eyes and imagine combining the parts to form a practical object or device that fit into the category.

  4. Judges rated each object for both practicality and originality.

      a. Practicality was equal for all three conditions.

      b. The most restrictive condition produced the most creative (both practical and original) products.

  5. In another experiment, subjects were assigned parts, told to create an object, and only then told what category the object had to fit into.

      a. Preassembled objects are called *preinventive forms*.

      b. This condition produced products that were even more creative than any of the conditions in the preceding experiment.

C. The Geneplore Model

  1. Generation strategy (e.g., imagine interesting combinations of parts, followed by

  2. Exploration strategy (in which a use for the imagined combination is sought.

CHAPTER 13: PRACTICE QUESTIONS (Answers and page references are on p. 177.)

Multiple Choice Questions: For each question, circle the single, best alternative.

1. Knowledge about a particular content area is called

   a. declarative knowledge.
   b. domain-general knowledge.
   c. domain-specific knowledge.
   d. procedural knowledge.

2. The two most dominant theories of expertise emphasize

   a. creative ability.
   b. experience and ability.
   c. multiple intelligences.
   d. production rules.

3. You are shown the cards "New York," "Los Angeles," "Car," and "Boat." You are told that each card has a city on side and a mode of transportation on the other. Which card(s) would you have to turn over to test the rule, "Every time I go to New York, I go by car?"

   a. New York only
   b. New York and Car
   c. New York and Boat
   d. all four cards

4. Griggs and Cox argue that the superior performance of British subjects on the letter-sorting version of the four-card selection problem is due to

   a. knowledge of permission schemas.
   b. knowledge of obligation schemas.
   c. recalling personal experiences.
   d. superior reasoning ability.

5. Cheng, Holyoak, Nisbett, and Oliver argue that that the superior performance of American college students on the drinking-age version of the four-card selection problem is due to

   a. knowledge of permission schemas.
   b. knowledge of obligation schemas.
   c. recalling personal experiences.
   d. superior reasoning ability.

6. When are people better at evaluating conditional statements? When they are

   a. about arbitrary relations
   b. about permission
   c. about obligations
   d. both *b* and *c*

7. Silver has shown that novices group problems according to

   a. inexplicable rules.
   b. solution procedure.
   c. surface characteristics.
   d. both *b* and *c*

8. When good problem solvers are asked to recall information about story problems, they recall

   a. details of story content.
   b. mathematical structure.
   c. irrelevant details.
   d. both *a* and *b*

9. In the experiment in which developmental and social psychology faculty who were not memory experts were asked to design a memory experiment, these faculty were considered to be

   a. domain experts.
   b. procedural experts.
   c. psychology experts.
   d. task experts.

10. In the experiment referred to in Problem 9, both memory experts and the developmental and social faculty members were better than undergraduates at

    a. domain-general skills.
    b. domain-specific skills.
    c. using the computer interface.
    d. all of the above

11. Gick's model of problem solving emphasizes the distinction between

    a. looking for and applying a solution.
    b. expert and novice problem solvers.
    c. constructing a problem representation and implementing a solution.
    d. all of the above

12. Solution search requires

    a. domain-general strategies.
    b. domain-specific strategies.
    c. expertise.
    d. production rules.

13. Planning is helpful in

    a. solving puzzle-like problems for the first time.
    b. solving the four-card problem.
    c. writing computer programs.
    d. designing alien creatures.

14. As individuals become more expert in a domain, they switch from

    a. means-end analysis to working forward.
    b. working forward to means-end analysis.
    c. relying on procedural knowledge to relying on declarative knowledge.
    d. both a and c

15. Although means-end analysis is efficient for _____ it is inefficient for _____.

    a. learning the solution sequence; obtaining the goal
    b. learning the solution sequence; reducing differences
    c. obtaining the goal; reducing differences
    d. obtaining the goal; learning the solution sequence

16. The "myth of genius" view argues that creativity

    a. occurs differently than other kinds of problem solving.
    b. results from sudden leaps of insight.
    c. results from ordinary thought processes.
    d. both a and b

17. Students who are shown examples of possible alien creatures and told not to copy them

    a. always follow the instructions.
    b. always end up producing similar creatures.
    c. only plagiarize the examples if they produce their own creatures immediately.
    d. only plagiarize the examples if they produce their own creatures after a 24-hour delay.

18. Creative solutions to design problems are produced more often when subjects are given

    a. maximum freedom in approaching the problem.
    b. intermediate freedom in approaching the problem.
    c. minimal freedom in approaching the problem.
    d. instructions to be creative.

19. The phrase "preinventive forms" refers to

    a. parts that haven't yet been combined.
    b. combinations of parts that haven't yet been categorized.
    c. early, discarded attempts that precede a creative combination of parts.
    d. both *a* and *b*

20. The Geneplore model suggests that ___ be placed on generation ___ exploration in the attempt to form creative products.

    a. greater emphasis; than on
    b. equal emphasis; and
    c. less emphasis; than on
    d. all the emphasis; and none on

True-False Questions:

T F   1.   The creativity of a product is determined by how original it is.

T F   2.   Sternberg believes that while expertise can be taught, ability is something you have to be born with.

T F   3.   American students were just as good at solving the letter-sorting version of the four-card selection problem as were British subjects.

T F   4.   The memory retrieval explanation of performance on the four-card selection problem asserts that people are better with concrete version of the problem because they don't have to reason to solve them.

T F   5.   Obligation schemata involve evaluating permission statements.

T F   6.   Expert problem solvers group problems based on solution procedures.

T F   7.   Knowledge about the specific hypothesis being tested is not relevant to designing a good experiment.

T F   8.   Schema activation may reduce the need to search for a solution.

T F   9.   Students assigned to a goal condition switched to a working forward strategy.

T F   10.   ACT* assumes that declarative knowledge has to be converted into production rules.

Essay Questions:

1. Explain why Cheng, Holyoak, Nisbett, and Oliver's view of reasoning is "more encouraging than the memory retrieval explanation proposed by Griggs and Cox."

2. Suppose that a friend has been assigned the task of designing a creative (both original and practical) long-term memory experiment. Based on what you learned from this chapter, what advice would you give your friend?

CHAPTER 14: DECISION MAKING

I. **Making Choices**
  A. **Compensatory Models**
    1. Allow attractive features to compensate for unattractive ones
    2. The *additive model* is a kind of compensatory model.
      a. Combines attractive and unattractive features to arrive at a total score for each alternative
      b. There are two ways of modifying the summation rule that could change the results.
        i. Weight features by importance.
        ii. Consider interactions among attributes.
    3. The *additive-difference model*: compares two alternatives by totaling the differences between values on each dimension.
    4. Although both models result in same decision, the search for information is different.
      a. The additive model evaluates all features of a single alternative before considering the next alternative.
      b. The additive-difference model compares two alternatives, attribute by attribute.
    5. Both are good procedures for evaluating alternatives.
    6. Both consider <u>all</u> attributes of each alternative and allow attractive attributes to compensate for unattractive ones.
  B. **Noncompensatory Models**
    1. Unattractive features result in the elimination of alternatives.
    2. Tversky (1972) has proposed that we make choices by gradually eliminating less attractive alternatives.
    3. This model is called *elimination by aspects* because it assumes that elimination is based on sequential evaluation of the features, or aspects, of the alternatives.
      a. If an attribute of an alternative does not satisfy some minimum criteria, that alternative is eliminated from the set of choices.
      b. Final choice depends on the order in which the features are considered.
      c. Therefore, model proposes that attributes differ in importance, and the probability of selecting a feature for consideration depends on its importance.
      d. Advantage over compensatory models = NO calculations
      e. Disadvantage = possible failure to find "best" alternative

4. The *conjunctive model* -- a variant of elimination-by-aspects -- requires that <u>all</u> aspects of an alternative meet some minimum criterion before that alternative can be selected.
   a. People finish evaluating one alternative before they begin considering the next.
   b. The first alternative that meets all of the minimum criteria is chosen (*satisficing search*).

C. Selecting a Strategy

1. Payne (1976) Presented information describing attributes of apartments, e.g., rent, cleanliness, noise level, etc.
   a. Information describing each apartment was printed on the back of an index card, which identified the dimension, e.g., rent.
   b. To get information, cards had to be turned over.
   c. Payne also asked people to think aloud as they evaluated information on cards.
   d. Students were given a variety of tasks that differed in the number of alternatives (2, 4, 8, or 12) as well as in the number of dimensions (4, 8, or 12) for which there was information about each alternative.
2. Payne proposed that search strategies could be classified along two dimensions:
   a. Whether search among dimensions was <u>constant </u>(same number of features considered for all alternatives) or <u>variable</u> (different numbers of features considered)
   b. Whether search was <u>intra</u>dimensional (considering same feature for several alternatives) or <u>inter</u>dimensional (considering all features of each alternative before considering next alternative)

SEARCH DIMENSION 2	SEARCH DIMENSION 1	
	Constant	Variable
Interdimensional	Additive-difference	Elimination-by-aspects
Intradimensional	Additive	Conjunctive

3. Results: students changed from searching a constant number of dimensions for two alternatives to a variable number of dimensions as the number of alternatives increased.
   a. In other words, for a small number of alternatives people used either the additive-difference or additive models and, for a larger number of alternatives, they used tended to either the elimination-by-aspects or conjunctive models.
   b. After several alternatives were eliminated, they reverted to compensatory models.

II. Estimating Probabilities
A. Kahneman and Tversky
1. We often base probability estimates on heuristics rather than on analytic procedures.
2. Sometimes these heuristics provide reasonable estimates of the probabilities involved, but most often they do not.
3. Two heuristics are *availability* and *representativeness*.

B. Availability: The Availability Heuristic proposes that we evaluate the probability of an event by judging the ease with which relevant instances come to mind.
1. When availability is highly correlated with actual frequencies, estimates should be accurate.
2. Other factors than frequency can affect availability judgments. When these conflict with frequency, the availability heuristic may result in systematic biases in estimating probabilities.
3. Slovic, Fischhoff, and Lichtenstein (1976) used the availability hypothesis to explain how people estimated the relative probability of 41 causes of death.
   a. They combined the 41 causes of death into 106 pairs. (Examples of the pairs are shown in Table 14.2, p. 361.)
   b. Students were asked to judge which member of a pair was the more likely cause of death.
   c. Ability to judge the likelihood of death varies greatly across the pairs.
   d. Examination of the events most seriously misjudged provided indirect support for the hypothesis that availability, particularly as influenced by the media, biases probability estimates.
      i. The frequencies of accidents, e.g., cancer, tornadoes, and botulism -- all of which receive heavy media coverage -- were greatly overestimated.
      ii. Asthma and diabetes, which receive less coverage, were underestimated.

C. **Representativeness:** The Representativeness Heuristic states that the probability of an event is estimated by evaluating how similar it is to a prototype.
   1. It's a "family resemblance" judgment of sorts.
   2. People ignore sample size when making probability estimates.
      a. For example, 600 boys in 1,000 was judged to be as likely as 60 in 100.
      b. Objectively, 60 in 100 is <u>much</u> more likely than 600 in 1,000.
   3. People tend to ignore prior probabilities and base their decisions only on the similarity between an instance and a concept.
      a. For example, half of a group of psychologists was told that 30 engineers and 70 lawyers had been given personality tests. The other half were told that 70 engineers and 30 lawyers had been tested.
      b. They were all given the same description (that sounded engineer-like) of one of the interviewed individuals and asked to estimate the probability that the individual was an engineer.
      c. Probability estimates were the same (and too high) for both groups.

III. **Combining Probabilities and Values**
   A. **A *normative* procedure for combining probabilities and values is called *expected value.***
      1. Like other normative models, expected value can be used as a standard of reference to evaluate decisions.
      2. Roll a die. If 5 or a 6 is rolled, you win $5. If one of other numbers appears, you lose. It costs $1 to play. Should you play?

      Expected value = P(Win) x V(Win) + P(Loss) x V(Loss)

      Expected value = $\frac{2}{6}$ x $4 + $\frac{4}{6}$ x -$1 = +$$\frac{4}{6}$

      3. A decision based on the normative model should be to play if expected value is positive and not to play for a negative expected value. In the above example, you can expect to win an average of 67¢ each time you take the gamble.
      4. Normative model fails as a descriptive model because it often fails to predict real behavior.

B. Expected Utility

1. One change in normative model is to substitute utility (a subjective assessment of value) into the expected value equation in place of objective value.
2. Suppose you enjoy gambling. Then the act of gambling has utility in addition to money won or lost. If you enjoy winning and don't mind losing, then you might formulate a positive expected utility for game described before. If U(W) = $6 and U(L) = -$1, then

   Expected utility = P(Win) x U(Win) + P(Loss) x U(Loss)

   Expected utility $= \frac{2}{6}$ x $6 $+ \frac{4}{6}$ x -$1 = $1\frac{2}{6}$

C. Subjective Expected Utility

1. A second change in the expected value model is to substitute subjective probabilities (which we know often don't match objective probabilities) into equation, e.g.,

   Subjective Expected Utility = SP(Win) x U(Win) + SP(Loss) x U(Loss)

   a. By substituting subjective values for the objective ones utilized in the expected value equation, we can do a better job of predicting people's decisions.
   b. However, this model places equal weight on all four factors entering into the decision, and people may not do that.
2. *Decision frame* affects probability judgments. If you're told that 97% of heart surgeries are successful, you're more likely to expect a positive outcome than if you're told that they fail 3% of the time, even though the probability of success is the same in both instances.

IV. Risk Dimensions

A. Importance of Risk Dimensions: Slovic and Lichtenstein's (1968) *duplex gambles*

1. They set up two spinners: the first determined whether the subject would win money, and the second whether the subject would lose money, e.g., the first spinner determines P(Win) = .4 and V(Win) = $1 while 2nd spinner determines P(Loss) = .2 and V(Loss) = $4.
2. There are four possible outcomes of this gamble: win $1 and lose $4 (net loss $3), win $1 and lose $0 (net gain $1), win $0 and lose $0 (net loss $0), and win $0 and lose $4 (net loss $4).

3. They used two methods to determine the attractiveness of a bet.
   a. Rating scale -5 (strong preference for not playing) to +5 (strong preference for playing)
   b. Second method required subjects to indicate largest amount of money they would be willing to pay experimenter to play the gamble (for attractive gambles) or in order not to have to play (for unattractive gambles).
4. Slovic and Lichtenstein correlated attractiveness of gamble with the four risk dimensions. If subjects consider all dimensions equally, correlations should be equal for all dimensions.
5. The results showed that the responses of most subjects were determined by the values on one or, at most, two dimensions and were unresponsive to changes in the values on the less important dimensions.
6. Data also showed that the particular dimension attended to was influenced by whether subjects responded with a numerical rating or a monetary response.

Percentage of subjects for whom a particular risk dimension was most important

	Risk Dimension			
	P(Win)	V(win)	P(Loss)	V(Loss)
Rating Group	50	9	15	26
Bidding Group	18	19	10	53

B. Perceived Risk:
1. The majority of individuals don't like taking risks.
2. Given a choice between winning $1 if a head comes up and losing $1 if a tail comes up and winning $100 if a head comes up and losing $100 if a tail comes up when a coin is flipped, many people will agree to gamble $1 but only a few will gamble $100 even though the expected value of the two bets is the same.

$$EV = P(Win) \times V(Win) + P(Loss) \times V(Loss)$$
$$= .5 \times \$1 + .5 \times -\$1$$
$$= 0$$
$$= .5 \times \$100 + .5 \times -\$100$$
$$= 0$$

V. Applications

A. Decision Aids and Training: physicians' probability estimates that a woman has breast cancer given that a mammogram was positive are more accurate when the data are presented as frequencies rather than as probabilities.

B. Jury Decision Making

1. May hear days or even weeks of testimony before being asked to make decision
2. Pennington and Hastie (1991; 2000) have proposed a story model (they view story construction as the jurors' main cognitive task) with three components:
   a. Evidence evaluation through story construction
   b. Representation of the decision alternates by verdict categories
   c. Reaching a decision by fitting the story into the best fitting verdict category
   d. Action/feedback loops
3. Similarities to text comprehension research:
   a. Role of prior knowledge
   b. Role of knowledge about story structures
4. Jury decisions are affected by the difficulty the jurors experience in constructing a coherent story (Pennington and Hastie, 1988).
5. Jurors bias their interpretation of new evidence toward whatever verdict they currently support.

C. Action-based Decision Making

1. Emergency situation characteristics:
   a. Ill-structured problems
   b. Uncertain dynamic environment
   c. Shifting or competing goals
   d. Action/feedback loops
   e. Time pressure
   f. High stakes
   g. Multiple participants
   h. Organizational goals that guide decision making
2. Recognition-primed decision model places emphasis on situational assessment and recognition of what's occurring.
   a. Expertise is a factor in both processes.
   b. Decision makers satisfice.

CHAPTER 14: PRACTICE QUESTIONS (Answers and page references are on p. 178.)

Multiple Choice Questions: For each question, circle the single, best alternative.

1. Benjamin Franklin's strategy for decision making is best described as a

   a. additive model.
   b. additive-difference model.
   c. elimination-by-aspects model.
   d. non-compensatory model.

2. A normative model

   a. describes how people behave.
   b. dictates how people should behave.
   c. is never compensatory.
   d. is never non-compensatory.

3. Decision making models that do not allow attractive attributes to make up for unattractive attributes are

   a. additive.
   b. compensatory.
   c. non-compensatory.
   d. normative.

4. Duplex gambles involve _____ probabilities of winning and losing.

   a. dependent
   b. independent
   c. doubling the
   d. halving the

5. In order to accurately estimate probabilities using Baye's theorem, you must know the

   a. expected value model.
   b. minimum criteria for satisficing.
   c. prior probabilities.
   d. subjective probabilities.

6. The utility of an outcome refers to its

   a. objective usefulness.
   b. objective desirability.
   c. subjective usefulness.
   d. subjective desirability.

7. Risky decision making occurs when

   a. the outcome is determined by the decision.
   b. the outcome is not determined by the decision.
   c. there's no decision frame.
   d. both *b* and *c*

8. If I buy the first washing machine that I see that is within my budget and has all of the wash cycles that I want, I am

   a. getting the best machine for my purposes.
   b. saving myself time.
   c. satisficing.
   d. both *b* and *c*

9. Most models of decision making consider only the

   a. decision event.
   b. objective value of outcomes.
   c. subjective probability of outcomes.
   d. subjective value of outcomes.

10. Models that attempt to depict how people behave are

   a. conjunctive models.
   b. descriptive models.
   c. noncompensatory models.
   d. normative models.

11. Determining an event's likelihood by the difficulty of bringing to mind similar events is an example of

   a. the availability heuristic.
   b. the representativeness heuristic.
   c. satisficing.
   d. a recognition-primed decision.

12. Asking oneself how similar an instance is to a prototype in order to make a probability judgment is an example of

   a. the availability heuristic.
   b. the representativeness heuristic.
   c. satisficing.
   d. a recognition-primed decision.

13. You refuse to consider further any exemplars in which not all attributes meet your minimum criteria. This is an example of

   a. satisficing.
   b. elimination-by-aspects.
   c. conjunctive decision making.
   d. subjective utility.

14. Payne has shown that people

    a. have a preferred decision strategy that they always use.
    b. choose a decision strategy that doesn't overload their information-processing capabilities.
    c. use additive-difference strategies most of the time.
    d. use compensatory strategies most of the time.

15. The order in which alternatives are considered affects the final decision for which of the following models?

    a. additive
    b. additive-difference
    c. conjunctive
    d. elimination-by-aspects

16. Decision frames affect

    a. objective probabilities.
    b. subjective probabilities.
    c. objective decisions.
    d. both a and c

17. People overestimate the probability of dying from various kinds of accidents, e.g., getting struck by lightening, because they

    a. can easily bring examples to mind.
    b. find the instances to be representative of the concept "accident."
    c. are confusing frequency with amount of media coverage.
    d. both a and c

18. People do not pay equal attention to the four risk dimensions. According to Slovic and Lichtenstein's research, when people rate gambles the dimension that receives the most attention is

    a. amount of a loss.
    b. amount of a win.
    c. probability of a loss.
    d. probability of a win.

19. The fact that people don't place equal weight on the four risk dimensions is difficult for ____ models to explain.

    a. compensatory
    b. non-compensatory
    c. descriptive
    d. normative

20. Difficulty in disentangling the prosecutor's evidence is likely to result in a jury finding a defendant

    a. guilty.
    b. not guilty.
    c. in contempt of the court.
    d. None of the above.

True-False Questions:

T F   1. Decision making can be grossly divided into two categories depending on whether outcome probabilities must be taken into account.

T F   2. Baye's theorem uses observed data to evaluate hypotheses.

T F   3. One way to improve medical decision making is to provide physicians with frequencies instead of probabilities.

T F   4. Waiting to see whether a cat can be coaxed out of a tree before sending someone to climb the tree to retrieve the cat is an example of an action/feedback loop.

T F   5. Successful recognition-primed decision making is usually the domain of experts.

T F   6. In emergency situations, most decision-makers satisfice.

T F   7. Fires and drowning are equally frequent causes of death.

T F   8. The expected value model combines subjective probabilities and values.

T F   9. The value you attach to an object depends on whether the object was earned or won in a random drawing.

T F   10. In general, many people enjoy taking risks.

STUDY GUIDE FOR REED'S COGNITION
CHAPTER 14: DECISION MAKING

Essay Questions:

1. Summarize the additive, additive-difference, conjunctive and elimination-by-aspects models of decision making. How do they differ?

2. How do normative and descriptive models of decision making differ? Give one example of each. (Make sure you indicate what makes the model either normative or descriptive.)

ANSWERS TO PRACTICE QUESTIONS

Format: Item number. Correct alternative (page reference)

Chapter 1:

Multiple Choice:
1. d (p. 2)
2. c (Figure 1.1, p. 3)
3. b (pp. 3-4)
4. c (p. 4)
5. a (p. 6)
6. a (p. 6)
7. c (p. 9)
8. a (pp. 10-11)
9. b (p. 4)
10. c (p. 10)
11. c (p. 5)
12. a (p.4)

True-False:
1. T (p. 3)
2. F (pp. 6-7)
3. F (pp. 5-6)
4. F (Fig. 1.1, p. 3)
5. F (pp. 3, 6-7)
6. T (p. 12)
7. T (p. 12)
8. T (p. 13)
9. T (pp. 8-9)
10. F (p. 6)
11. F (p. 4)

Chapter 2:

Multiple Choice:
1. b (p. 22)
2. d (p. 24)
3. a (p. 32)
4. a (p. 30)
5. d (p. 35)
6. a (p. 20)
7. c (pp. 26-27)
8. c (p. 27)
9. a (pp. 25-26)
10. c (p. 26)
11. b (p. 28)
12. a (pp. 31-32)
13. a (p. 30)
14. c (p. 31)
15. d (p. 32)
16. b (p. 34)
17. a (pp. 36-37)
18. c (Fig. 2.14, p. 36)
19. c (p. 39)
20. b (p. 39)
21. c (p. 26)
22. b. (p.17)
23. d (p.28)
24. b (p.28)
25. d (p.36)

True-False:
1. F (p. 29)
2. T (p. 37)
3. F (p. 36)
4. F (p. 36)
5. T (p. 32)
6. T (p. 37)
7. F (p. 42)
8. F (p. 44)
9. T (p. 28)
10. F (p. 22)
11. T (p.24)

STUDY GUIDE FOR REED'S COGNITION
ANSWERS TO PRACTICE QUESTIONS

Chapter 3:

Multiple Choice:
1. a (p. 48)
2. c (p. 48)
3. d (p. 50)
4. c (p. 56)
5. b (p. 53)
6. b (p. 54)
7. d (p. 44)
8. a (p. 44)
9. b (p. 48)
10. c (p. 48)
11. a (p. 49)
12. c (p. 49)
13. d (Fig. 3.4, p. 51)
14. b (p. 58)
15. b (p. 54)
16. b (p. 56)
17. c (p. 56)
18. b (p. 60)
19. c (p. 62)
20. c (pp. 58-59)
21. b (p.64)
22. c (p. 61)

True-False:
1. F (pp. 52, 61)
2. F (p. 65)
3. T (p. 56)
4. F (p. 57)
5. F (p. 56)
6. F (p. 58)
7. T (p. 61)
8. T (p. 63)
9. F (pp. 66-67)
10. F (pp. 73-74)

Chapter 4:

<u>Multiple Choice</u>:
1. a (p. 78)
2. b (p. 89)
3. a (p. 77)
4. b (p. 81)
5. c (Fig. 4.2, pp. 71-72)
6. a (p. 81)
7. a (Fig. 4.8, p. 87)
8. c (Fig. 4.4, p. 75)
9. c (p. 74)
10. c (p. 81)
11. a (p. 83)
12. c (p. 76)
13. c (p. 81)
14. b (p. 82)
15. b (p. 84)
16. a (p. 85)
17. c (p. 88)
18. b (p. 88)
19. d (p. 89)
20. a (p. 77-78)
21. b (p. 92)
22. b (p. 93)

<u>True-False</u>:
1. F (p. 73)
2. F (Fig. 4.3, p. 73)
3. T (Fig. 4.4, p. 75)
4. F (p. 76)
5. F (p. 78)
6. T (pp. 82-84)
7. T (Fig. 4.8, p. 87)
8. F (p. 93)
9. F (p. 89)
10. F (pp. 70, 88)

STUDY GUIDE FOR REED'S COGNITION
ANSWERS TO PRACTICE QUESTIONS

Chapter 5:

Multiple Choice:
1. a (p. 103)
2. b (Fig. 5.2, p. 102)
3. b (pp. 102-103)
4. c (p. 117)
5. d (p. 106)
6. c (Fig. 5.2, p. 102)
7. c (p. 98)
8. c (p. 100-101)
9. d (p. 101)
10. a (Fig. 5.2, p. 102)
11. a (p. 106)
12. b (p. 106)
13. c (p. 109) Note: UNfamiliar words do not produce TOT
14. c (p. 114)
15. d (p. 115)
16. c (p. 116)
17. c (p. 118)
18. b (p. 118)
19. c (p. 99)
20. c (p. 105)
21. a (108)
22. c (p. 112)
23. d (Table 5.1, p. 113)
24. c (Table 5.1, p. 113)
25. a (p. 115)

True-False:
1. T (p. 110)
2. T (p. 98)
3. F (p. 105)
4. F (p. 115)
5. F (pp. 109-110)
6. F (Fig. 5.2, p. 102)
7. F (p. 107)
8. F (p. 106)
9. T (p. 111)
10. F (p. 120)

Chapter 6:

Multiple Choice:
1. c (p. 132)
2. b (p. 143)
3. b (Table 6.3, p. 144)
4. b (p. 139)
5. c (p. 143)
6. b (p. 134)
7. d (Fig. 6.2, 134)
8. b (p. 137)
9. d (p. 136)
10 b (p. 146)
11. b (p. 144)
12. b (p. 127)
13. b (p. 129)
14. c (p. 135)
15. a (Table 6.3, p. 144)
16. c (p. 143)
17. b (p. 132)
18. b (p. 129)
19. c (pp. 145-146)
20. b (p. 148)

True-False:
1. T (p. 126)
2. F (p. 131)
3. T (p. 132)
4. T (p. 135)
5. F (p. 132)
6. F (p. 133)
7. T (p. 132)
8. F (p. 133)
9. F (p. 140)
10. T (p. 139)

Chapter 7:

Multiple Choice:
1. b (Fig. 7.5, p. 165)
2. a (p. 164)
3. b (p. 157)
4. b (p. 157)
5. a (p. 157)
6. a (p. 170)
7. b (p. 161)
8. c (p. 156)
9. c (p. 158-159)
10. b (p. 157)
11. d (p. 164)
12. c (Fig. 7.2, p. 157)
13. d (p. 178)
14. b (p. 180)
15. d (pp. 175-176)
16. b (p. 173)
17. c (p. 172)
18. a (p. 171)
19. d (p. 169)
20. b (pp. 174-176)

True-False:
1. F (p. 154)
2. F (pp. 156-159)
3. F (p. 158)
4. T (p. 159)
5. F (p. 160)
6. F (p. 160)
7. T (p. 162)
8. F (p. 164)
9. F (p. 173)
10. T (p. 174)

Chapter 8:

<u>Multiple Choice</u>:
1. c (p. 202)
2. d (p. 197)
3. c (p. 187)
4. a (p. 204)
5. c (pp. 195-197)
6. b (Table 8.5, pp. 195-196)
7. d (p. 190)
8. d (p. 197)
9. c (p. 186)
10. b (p. 187)
11. a (p. Fig. 8.2, p. 191)
12. d (pp. 208-109)
13. b (p. 194)
14. b (pp. 190, 197)
15. b (p. 206)
16. c (p. 208)
17. d (p. 209)
18. b (p. 205)
19. b (Table 8.5, p. 196)
20. c (p. 190)

<u>True-False</u>:
1. T (p. 186)
2. T (Fig. 8.2, p. 209)
3. F (p. 187)
4. T (p. 189)
5. F (Table 8.3, p. 192)
6. F (pp. 194-195)
7. T (p. 201)
8. F (p. 205)
9. F (p. 205)
10. F (pp. 206-207)

STUDY GUIDE FOR REED'S COGNITION
ANSWERS TO PRACTICE QUESTIONS

Chapter 9:

Multiple Choice:
1. a (Fig. 9.7, p. 228)
2. b (p. 228)
3. b (Fig. 9.2, p. 216)
4. b (p. 217)
5. a (p. 220)
6. a (p. 219)
7. b (p. 220)
8. b (Fig. 9.5, p. 222)
9. d (p. 222)
10. c (Fig. 9.6, p. 223)
11. d (pp. 225-226)
12. c (p. 225)
13. a (p. 225)
14. c (Fig. 9.5, p. 222; Fig. 9.7, p. 228)
15. a (pp. 228-229)
16. c (p. 233)
17. d (p. 234)
18. d (p. 236)
19. c (p. 237)
20. a (p. 240)

True-False:
1. T (p. 228)
2. T (p. 225)
3. F (p. 218)
4. T (Fig. 9.5, p. 222)
5. T (pp. 228-229)
6. F (pp. 231, 236)
7. F (p. 225)
8. F (p. 233)
9. T (p. 234)
10. T (p. 238)

Chapter 10:

<u>Multiple Choice</u>:
1. a (p. 246)
2. a (Fig. 10.1, p. 247)
3. d (p. 248)
4. a (p. 249)
5. b (p. 245)
6. a (p. 253-254)
7. d (p. 257)
8. c (p. 252)
9. d (pp. 260-261)
10. c (p. 265)
11. d (p. 246)
12. c (p. 251)
13. d (p. 252)
14. a (p. 254)
15. d (Fig. 10.6, p. 259)
16. d (p. 261)
17. b (p. 262)
18. d (p. 268)
19. b (Fig. 10.2, pp. 246-247)
20. c (p. 252)

<u>True-False</u>:
1. F (p. 268)
2. F (p. 248)
3. T (pp. 249-250)
4. T (p. 253)
5. F (p. 264)
6. T (p. 264)
7. F (p. 262)
8. F (p. 261)
9. F (p. 267)
10. T (p. 267)

STUDY GUIDE FOR REED'S COGNITION
ANSWERS TO PRACTICE QUESTIONS

Chapter 11:

Multiple Choice:
1. d (p. 292-294)
2. b (p. 276)
3. c (pp. 276-277)
4. c (Fig. 11.2, p. 280)
5. a (pp. 278-279)
6. c (p. 281)
7. b (p. 281)
8. d (p. 281)
9. c (p. 283)
10. a (p. 283)
11. a (p. 285)
12. d (p. 285)
13. d (p. 286)
14. d (pp. 281, 293)
15. c (p. 288)
16. c (p. 291)
17. c (p. 291)
18. b (p. 293)
19. d (p. 293)
20. d (p. 196)

True-False:
1. T (p. 293)
2. F (p. 276-277)
3. T (p. 278-279)
4. F (Fig. 11.2, p. 280)
5. F (p. 281)
6. F (p. 282)
7. T (p. 285)
8. F (p. 291)
9. T (p. 289)
10. T (pp. 290-291)

Chapter 12:

<u>Multiple Choice</u>:
1. b (p. 313)
2. a (p. 310)
3. a (p. 305)
4. c (p. 313)
5. c (p. 305)
6. c (p. 301)
7. b (p. 302)
8. a (p. 305)
9. b (p. 304)
10. a (p. 304)
11. a (pp. 305-306)
12. c (p. 308)
13. c (p. 309)
14. b (p. 310)
15. b (pp. 311-312)
16. d (p. 312)
17. b (p. 312)
18. b (p. 316)
19. c (p. 314)
20. b (p. 324)
21. d (p. 324)

<u>True-False</u>:
1. T (pp. 303-304)
2. F (p. 307)
3. T (pp. 312-313)
4. T (p. 310)
5. F (p. 311)
6. T (p. 312)
7. F (p. 312)
8. T (p. 316)
9. T (pp. 318-319)
10. F (p. 322)

Chapter 13:

<u>Multiple Choice:</u>
1. c (p. 330)
2. b (p. 330)
3. c (p. 332)
4. c (p. 333)
5. a (pp. 333-334)
6. d (p. 334)
7. c (p. 335)
8. b (p. 336)
9. d (p. 337)
10. a (Fig. 13.2, p.337)
11. d (Fig. 13.3, p. 338)
12. a (p. 339)
13. c (pp. 339-340)
14. a (p. 340)
15. d (p. 341)
16. c (p. 343-344)
17. d (p. 346)
18. c (p. 347)
19. b (p. 347)
20. b (p. 348)

<u>True-False:</u>
1. F (p. 343)
2. F (p. 330)
3. F (p. 333)
4. T (p. 333)
5. F (p. 334)
6. T (pp. 335-336)
7. F (pp. 337-338)
8. T (Fig. 13.3, p. 338)
9. F (p. 341)
10. T (p. 342)

Chapter 14:

<u>Multiple Choice</u>:
1. a (pp. 354-355)
2. b (p. 354)
3. c (p. 356)
4. b (p. 368)
5. c (Fig. 14.3, p. 372)
6. d (p. 365)
7. b (p. 354)
8. d (p. 357)
9. a (p. 376)
10. b (p. 354)
11. a (p. 360)
12. b (p. 362)
13. b (p. 356)
14. b (pp. 357-358)
15. d (p. 356)
16. b (p. 366)
17. d (pp. 360-361)
18. b (p. 369)
19. d (p. 369)
20. b (p. 375)

<u>True-False</u>:
1. T (p. 359)
2. T (p. 372)
3. T (p. 373)
4. T (p. 377)
5. T (p. 377)
6. T (p. 377)
7. T (Table 14.2, p. 361)
8. F (p. 365)
9. T (p. 366)
10. F (pp. 370-371)